The Sea
for Meaning
and Values

Patrick McManus

Writers: Pau
Colette McC

Series Coord
Micheál De

VERITAS

Published 2004 by
Veritas Publications
7-8 Lower Abbey Street
Dublin 1

ISBN 978-1-85390-861-3
Copyright © 2004 Irish Episcopal Commission on Catechetics

10 9 8 7 6 5 4

The writers and the editor would like to acknowledge the Religious Education teachers and students who piloted draft versions of this text and helped enormously with their feedback and comments. They would also like to thank the Post-Primary Diocesan Advisers for their invaluable help and support.

Theological Adviser: Patrick Mullins, O.Carm., STL
Consultant to the Series: Maura Hyland
Art Director: Bill Bolger
Text Editor: Elaine Campion
Typesetting: Paula Ryan
Picture Research: Helen Carr
Text Copyright Research: Majella Cullinane
Printed in Ireland by W & G Baird, Antrim

Acknowledgements

Ancient markings at Newgrange, Co. Meath, cover, © Eamonn Farrell, 1999; fans at Slane Castle, pp 6 & 8 © Gareth Chaney, 2003; Ground Zero, p 13, © Jean Catuffe; children dress up in costumes and enjoy Hallowe'en night in Dublin's Dolphin's Barn, 51, © Gareth Chaney, 2001; Newgrange, p 56, © Eamonn Farrell, 1999; photo of pilgrims' bare feet on Croagh Patrick, Co. Mayo, p 62, © Leon Farrell, 2002; and photo of Mary Robinson, p 123, © Gareth Chaney, 2002; all Photocall Ireland; used with permission. Photo of Newgrange (interior), title page, © Irish Times; used with permission. Photo of Fire Department chaplain, p 14, from Light at Ground Zero by Krystyna Sanderson (Square Halo Books, 2003). Photos of Justine and Gatera, Rwanda, p 17, © Trócaire and Noel Gavin/Allpix. 'Socrates accepting a cup of hemlock', p 24, illustration by Walter Crane in The Story of Greece by Mary Macgregor © Mary Evans/Edwin Wallace; engraving of Plato based on bust in the Uffizi Gallery, Florence, p 26; detail from 'Aristotle tutoring Alexander the Great' (Figuier, Les Savants Celebres), p 29; St Augustine of Hippo (Tiron Ordres Religieux, reproduced in 1848, Vol I), p 32; René Descartes from an engraving by J. Chapman, p 35; unattributed photograph of Friedrich Nietzsche, p 38, all © Mary Evans Picture Library; used with permission. Cuneiform clay tablet showing Gilgamesh story, p 47, and relief of Temple of the Sun-god, p 48, both © the British Museum. Photo, p 61, by Bill Doyle from Island Funeral (Veritas, 2000). Lough Derg, p 63, by Valerie O'Sullivan; used with permission. Photo of Taizé Meditation, p 64, by S. Leutnegger © Ateliers et Presses de Taizé, F-71250 Taizé-Communauté; used with permission. Photo of the Hubble Space Telescope, p 76, courtesy of the European Space Agency. 'The Rublev Icon', p 91, from Trinity Cathedral of the St Sergius' Trinity Monastery in Sergiev Posad. 'The Creation of Adam' by Michelangelo; detail from the Sistine Chapel, p 101.

Scripture quotations are taken from the New Revised Standard Version Bible; Catholic Edition © 1993 and 1998 by the Division of Christian Education of the National Council of the Churches of Christ in the United States of America. Songs 'Perfect' by Alanis Morisette (Maverick Music); 'I Still Haven't Found What I'm Looking For' by U2 (Island Records); 'Family Portrait' by Pink (Laface Records); 'From a Distance' by Nanci Griffith (MCA Records); 'Redemption Song' by Bob Marley (Island Records). The lines from The Great Hunger and 'Advent' by Patrick Kavanagh are reprinted by kind permission of the Trustees of the Estate of the late Katherine B. Kavanagh, through the Jonathan William Literary Agency. 'The Concerned Adolescent' by Wendy Cope (Faber and Faber). Poem from The Hour of the Unexpected by John Shea (Argos Communications, 1977). Quote from Anam Cara by John O'Donohue, published by Bantam Press; used with permission of the Random House Group Limited. Several extracts from Sophie's World by Jostein Gaarder (Orion Books, 1997).

Contents

Part Three: Concepts of God

Part Four: Religion and the Emergence of Values

I see it well: my mind will never be at peace,
till that Truth dawn upon it which hides
no further truth beyond itself.

Arriving there the mind will rest at last
like a wild beast at home within its lair;
and that arrival must be possible, unless
desire is doomed to mere frustration.

Meanwhile doubt upon doubt arise,
like off-shoots from the foot of truth;
it is our nature that such questions spur us
from hill to hill onward towards the summit.

Dante, Paradiso, IV, 124-132

Part One: The Quest for Meaning

Chapter 1: The Contemporary Context

Since the beginning of time, it seems that human beings have engaged with each other and with their world in the search for meaning. Human progress and scientific discovery have provided answers to some of what was mysterious to our ancient ancestors, yet the search for meaning in life continues today. People engage in this search at different times in their lives; often it is in times of crisis or great change that we ask: what is it all about? Why are we here? What is the significance of our relationships with others? What is our place in the cosmos? Is there a God? What things give meaning to our lives?

The search goes on, the questions are still being asked. Each individual must face these questions, as must each community and generation. Later in this text we will look at how people in the past searched for and found meaning in their lives, but we will begin by looking at some examples from contemporary culture, especially youth culture, for evidence of the search for meaning in our world today. According to the publication **Youth 2K**, **culture** 'is not something that we have, as in owning possessions. It is like the air we breathe, something we are part of...'.[1] What does the music, art and literature of contemporary culture tell us about the concerns of young people today?

The Search for Meaning in Modern Music

Contemporary music explores the high and low points of life. Many people find music a source of entertainment but also a source of comfort. Music expresses many of the feelings and anxieties experienced by people at different times in their lives. One of the central concerns of modern music, indeed of all music, is love; from falling in love to lost love, family love, friendship and love of self – music touches on them all. Read and/or listen to this excerpt from Alanis Morisette's song 'Perfect':

If you're flawless, then you'll win my love.
Don't forget to win first place.
Don't forget to keep that smile on your face.
Be a good girl.
You've gotta try a little harder.
That wasn't fast enough to make us happy.
We'll love you just the way you are if you're perfect.

Whose point of view is represented in this song?

What experience is being described?

According to the song, what effect has this experience of family life on the child?

Pink, in her song 'Family Portrait', describes a dysfunctional family situation:

Mama please stop cryin'.
I can't stand the sound.
Your pain is painful
And it's tearing me down.
I hear glasses breaking
As I sit up in my bed.
I told God you didn't mean
Those nasty things you said.
You fight about money,
About me and my brother.
And this I come home to.
This is my shelter.

It ain't easy growin' up in WW3,
Never knowin' what love could be.
You'll see, I don't want love to destroy me
Like it has done my family.

Music also celebrates the power of relationships and their influence in our lives.

Assignment
Explore modern music as an expression of the search for meaning by using examples from the music you listen to and find meaningful.

One of the areas of greatest concern for many people today is finding their place in the world. We spend much of our lives trying to understand who we are and what our purpose is in life. Part of this search for meaning involves coming to know and love ourselves.

> I have run, I have crawled,
> I have scaled these city walls,
> These city walls,
> Only to be with you.
>
> But I still haven't found
> What I'm looking for.
> But I still haven't found
> What I'm looking for.

(U2, 'I Still Haven't Found What I'm Looking For', from the *Joshua Tree* album)

The experience of suffering and loss forces us to ask questions and sometimes to change direction.

Assignment

Choose one or more songs that you think express something important about relationships or any dimension of the search for meaning. In relation to each one:

1.   What is the song about?
2.   Pick one image/line that you think is particularly effective and explain your choice.
3.   Does the artist suggest any answer/solution to the issue(s) raised? Explain.

Suggestions for further analysis:

Bob Dylan:	Every Grain of Sand
	The Times They Are a Changing
	Blowing in the Wind
U2:	Stuck in a Moment
	I Still Haven't Found what I'm Looking For
Nirvana:	Smells like Teen Spirit
	Dumb
Beatles:	Let it Be
	All You Need is Love
	Help

Poetry as a Vehicle for Meaning

The search for meaning is also expressed in literature and art. The literature of any culture includes all the types of written works you can imagine: drama, fiction, biography, poetry. Poetry in particular provides us with a medium through which many of the great questions of life are explored. Some of the poets that are studied in school, like Elizabeth Bishop and Seamus Heaney, deal with important issues such as family life, death, immortality, suffering and love. From ancient times to the present day, people have used poetry as a means of expressing their search for meaning. Poets have the ability to communicate the concerns of the society in which they live.

Niall MacMonagle tells us:

> Some poems can seem to be a million miles away from us… and others tell us exactly how it is. We identify; we say, yes, that's how it is for me.

Read this poem and answer the questions that follow.

The Concerned Adolescent

Our planet spins around the sun
in its oval shaped orbit
like a moth circling a bright, hot, golden yellow lightbulb.
Look at this beautiful, lovely
blue and green and white jewel
shining against the dark black sky.
It is doomed.
On another planet somewhere far away in the galaxy
beings are discussing the problems of Earth.
'It is a wonderful world,' says their leader,
'it has roaring oceans filled with many kinds of fishes,
it has green meadows bedecked with white and yellow flowers,
its trees have twisting roots and fruitful, abundant branches.
But it is doomed.'
'The problem with this lovely, beautiful world, you see,
is the inhabitants, known as HUMAN BEINGS
Human beings will not live in peace and love
and care for the little helpless creatures who
share the planet with them.
They pollute the world, they kill and eat the
animals.
Everywhere there is blood and the stench of
death.
Human beings make war and hate one another.
They do not understand their young, they reject
their ideals,

they make them come home early from the disco.
They are doomed.'
Soon a great explosion, a terrible cloud,
will wipe out all the life on this planet,
including those people who do not see how important
my poem is.
They are certainly doomed.
  Wendy Cope[3]

1. What issues are being explored in this poem?
2. What image of the world is being portrayed?
3. What does the poet say about human beings in general and
 young people in particular?
4. What is your response to this poem?

Assignment
From the list of poems you are studying for your Leaving Certificate
English examination, choose one or more that you think deal with
important questions, for example, they might explore suffering,
death, love, growing up, family, the past, etc. Write a note on each
poem and the issue(s) it explores. Comment on your own response
to the poem(s).

Resources for further
study
See teacher's text on
CD-Rom for further
suggestions.

Music, art and literature can reveal the concerns of the society in
which they were created. However, it is not just artists and writers
who look for meaning in life; we all do. It is in our nature as
human beings to look for meaning and to try to understand our
place in the world. People express their beliefs about life and their
own sense of who they are in a variety of ways. People make
choices about the way they dress, how they live, the job they do, the
way they spend their money or their time.

As Tom Beaudoin says of **Generation X:**

  *Like the sleeves we tore from our shirts, the Flashdance fashions also
  symbolised how ripped-off we felt as a generation. The ripped fashions
  signified the hard living we never had, the rough-and-tumble experiences
  (now frequently romanticised) like the Vietnam War that were not ours.[4]*

Many of the 'choices' a person makes every day can reveal
something about what they believe to be important or significant.
Our lifestyle can be a reflection of what we find meaningful.

Key Questions of Life

In our search for meaning and values, certain experiences and
events force us to question more deeply.

Then one of those phone calls was to change our lives forever. Johnny ran to say that he had been to the hospital for tests because he hadn't been feeling too well lately and he was awaiting the results. He wasn't one to worry about his health, so the fact that he had actually rung to tell us about this sounded ominous.

He phoned again when the results arrived. Non-Hodgkin's Lymphoma—fancy title that pronounced a death sentence on him. Had it been diagnosed four or five years earlier, the specialists told him, they'd have had a better chance, but they told him that, between them, he and they were going to kick it.[5]

Group Work

Give an example of what you consider to be a key question – a question that will face us all at one time or another. Perhaps someone has experienced a time when they asked 'why?' Note the responses of the students in your group on a large sheet of paper. Keep this sheet of paper for later use.

There are some key questions that are common to all people:

What is the goal and purpose of life?

At some point every person wonders: why am I here? Does my life have purpose? Is there a God? Whatever the answer to these questions, the very act of asking them has a fundamental effect on a person's approach to life. Different cultures have answered these questions in different ways. Each individual deals with these questions in his or her own way.

What is the meaning and purpose of suffering?

Despite all the advances in our world, we still have suffering. The struggle to understand suffering is common to all people. Sickness, death, crime, violence, natural disasters, discrimination and injustice of all kinds force us to ask: why does this happen? What does it mean? Individuals ask: Why me?

What is the nature of good and evil? How do we decide what is good and what is evil?

This is a question that emerges in every civilisation. Each culture develops its understanding of these positive and negative forces. Each individual must develop his or her own moral code. Is evil an inevitable part of life? Does good always triumph over evil?

The following story is an account of one woman's struggle to come to terms with the suffering and loss experienced by those who survived the terrorist attacks in New York on 11 September 2001. Kathleen Murphy is an Irish nurse who has lived in the United States for the past thirty years. On that fateful day in September 2001 she was working in a New York City hospital. The hospital was on full alert for the expected casualties, but no one arrived. Kathleen's experience of powerlessness in the face of such terrible suffering caused her great pain. Later, however, she found a way to remember and honour the New York firefighters who were killed on that day. Her story tells us something about the bond that is created between people through the experience of suffering, and

Identify other examples in contemporary culture of the key questions of life. In doing this you may look to contemporary music, art and literature. Each group could also examine national/ international events to see if they raise any or all of these questions. Perhaps these questions have touched the lives of individual members of the group.

1. Which key question of life is explored in the example you have chosen?
2. How is this question expressed?
3. What answer(s) is offered?
4. What is your response to these questions?

about the human quest to make sense of and cope with suffering and loss.

The events of 11 September 2001 also raise questions about good and evil.

Read the story and answer the questions that follow.

On September 11, I was working in the outpatient unit of a Manhattan hospital in New York City. The unit is also used as a backup for the emergency room if there is a crisis. When the World Trade Center Towers collapsed, we immediately sent home the patients from the outpatient unit because they were not in critical need. Patients in the hospital who were well enough to go home were also discharged. We thought we would need the space for what we expected to be a huge influx of emergency patients from the disaster. We were anticipating a crisis. We waited and waited. But as the day wore on, nobody came. A group of out-of-town nurses who were attending a meeting at a hotel in the city, left their meeting and went to hospitals around the city. They wanted to help, but there was nothing for them to do either...

Long ago my grandfather bought some land in Kinsale, County Cork, Ireland. The property has been in our family since the 1800s and four generations of my family have lived there. I own a little part of that land. It's where I was born, so it's really home and very

special to me. I wouldn't sell it for all the tea in China. Some time ago, I thought about planting a tree for each of my grandparents and their children on my part of the property. I love trees. They are a living symbol that continues on even after we're gone. They will be there for future generations to visit. After September 11, I decided to plant trees on my land for the firefighters who had been lost. At first I thought about just planting trees for the firefighters from the two firehouses located on each side of my home in Queens and for the two firehouses on each side of the hospital where I work. But one day when I was on Fifth Avenue and saw some of the firefighters' families, I knew I needed to plant one for each firefighter – not just the ones in the stations near me. That meant there would eventually be 343 trees.

A lot of the firefighters who died were young men with small children. Some of the children were not even born when their fathers were lost. Some children might not remember their fathers. I thought it would be nice for the children to be able to visit the trees that were planted for their fathers, especially those with Irish heritage. I think all of us search for our roots, no matter who we are or where we come from. The trees might be healing or helpful for the children, the families and co-workers of the firefighters. We chose the evergreen oak and a selection of other evergreen trees appropriate to the area. We know we can call the Fire Department at any time; they are always present twenty-four hours a day.

Evergreen trees are alive year round and would be symbolic of the ever-present firefighters. We wanted the trees to be planted on an area of the property where people could have easy access to them from the road; if people want to see the trees, they can just walk onto the property. We decided that the name of the firefighter and the company name would be placed on each tree, and that trees representing firefighters from the same company would stand close together. The community spirit around the tree-planting has been wonderful. My brother, who lives on the property, selected and ordered the trees. Local people with machinery came to dig the holes for the trees. A retired Kinsale firefighter asked some pipers and drummers to play, and made sure the fire trucks and fire department were at the ceremony. On 20 November 2001 it was freezing cold, but the whole community made sure the first forty-six trees were planted. One of the neighbours, who had grown an oak tree from an acorn, delivered it to the site that morning. It was planted for Fr Mychal Judge. There were prayers and music and the priest blessed all the trees. The town fathers made speeches and asked that their condolences be conveyed to the families in New York. Then neighbours, friends and family helped plant the trees. That night a special Mass for the firefighters was said in Kinsale.

The next group of eighty-six trees was planted on 2 March 2002. That, too, turned out to be a very special event. Three fire engines came from Kinsale, Carrigaline and Charleville, and the firefighters wore their uniforms. We had a singer, bagpipes and drums on the site. The grandfather of a firefighter who died at the World Trade Center came and planted a tree for his only grandson – the end of his family name. Also the aunt and uncle of another firefighter planted a tree for their nephew, who had been in Ireland the previous summer playing Irish music on the accordion. As they planted the tree and put his photo on it, they were crying. It was a sad but healing event for those families and a deeply moving time for all of us.

Families have contacted me and said how grateful they are for the trees, that they appreciate having a living memorial in Ireland for their missing loved ones. One family said their dad loved the outdoors and that he would have loved the trees. Recently I learned that one of the firefighters had been in Kinsale on vacation with his wife the summer before 9/11, and now we have planted a tree for him.[6]

Questions

1. Where was Kathleen Murphy working on 11 September 2001?
2. 'We waited and waited. But…nobody came.' Why was this?
3. What was Kathleen Murphy's response to the events of 11 September 2001?
4. What do you think Kathleen Murphy values in life? Give reasons for your answer.
5. What do you think the planting of the trees symbolises?
6. Can you think of other responses to the events of 11 September 2001?
7. Think of another example of suffering and comment on the ways in which people respond.

Assignment

Using newspapers, magazines, television and the Internet, research what you consider to be an example of evil in our world today. Describe your choice. Identify the various reasons why you consider this to be an example of evil. Identify the responses to this situation. Comment on the 'cause' of this evil. Present your findings to the class.

Factors that Block the Search for Meaning

While it is a natural instinct to ask these key questions and to engage in the search for meaning, it is not always possible to do so. There are obstacles that hinder the search for meaning. Before people can begin to reflect on the goal and purpose of life, on the nature of good and evil, and on the reason for suffering, they must first have their basic needs met. The psychologist Abraham Maslow outlined what he called the **'hierarchy of needs'** experienced by human beings:

Need for self-actualisation

Need for esteem

Need for belonging and love

Safety needs

Physical needs

Physical needs include food, water, air and shelter, basic requirements for survival. Safety needs refer to the need for security and protection and freedom from fear and anxiety. Belonging needs mean the need to feel a sense of belonging to a group and to have the opportunity to give and receive affection. The fourth level of need, the need for esteem, represents the need to be respected by others and to have a sense of self-respect, achievement and independence. Finally, the highest level of need, the need for self-actualisation, is the need to achieve a sense of self-fulfilment and to feel that we are in the process of becoming the persons that we are capable of becoming.

These needs are arranged in order of priority. So, it is only when our basic needs are met that we can begin to consider the next level of needs. If a person is suffering from hunger and lack of shelter, then they will not be in a position to attend to safety or belonging needs; they must first satisfy their immediate need of food and shelter. Likewise, it is only when the safety/security needs are met that a person can deal with the next level.

This topic is also considered in **Section D, Moral Decision-Making** and **Section F, Issues of Justice and Peace**.

Even when all these basic needs are met, there are other factors in society that hinder our search for meaning and prevent us from reflecting on the deep questions of life, for example, consumerism, work, exhaustion, affluence, apathy and disillusionment.

Questions

1. What are the most basic human needs?
2. Why is it not possible for a person to fulfil the need for self-actualisation if their basic need for food and shelter is not being met?
3. Barnardos, a leading children's charity, ran an advertising campaign with the slogan 'I am not hungry to succeed, I am hungry'. What issue was this campaign attempting to highlight?

Resources for further study
See teacher's text on CD-Rom for further suggestions.

'Justine is forty-five years old. Her husband was killed during the genocide of 1994. She never recovered his body and still doesn't know who killed him. She had two sons – Eugene and Gatera. Eugene died from cholera when he was fifteen. Gatera is now thirteen and is no longer going to school, as he needs to help his mother with the work. She calls this a 'sign of our poverty'. (Trócaire, Rwanda – A Case Study)

We live in a world that can discourage us from looking for meaning in places other than the prepackaged world offered by **consumerism**. We are bombarded by seductive messages that promise happiness and meaning if we buy this product, drive that car or wear those clothes. Success, wealth and beauty do not hold the answers to the deep questions of life. If these questions are not attended to or if they are avoided, problems will arise at a personal level and within society in general.

We are all too aware of the blight of drug abuse, alcohol abuse, violence, crime and sexual promiscuity in society. The increase in suicide, depression and eating disorders, especially among young people, indicates a deep level of unhappiness. These problems reveal to us that at some level the search for meaning has been hindered.

Exam fears driving teenagers to Prozac
(*The Observer*, 6 June 2004)

Plea for price rise to reduce alcohol abuse
(The *Irish Times*, 4 June 2004)

Say goodbye to Sunday, day of rest
(Sunday *Times*, 6 June 2004)

1. In groups, choose one of the factors listed below which block the search for meaning.

- Group 1: Consumerism
- Group 2: Work
- Group 3: Exhaustion
- Group 4: Affluence
- Group 5: Apathy
- Group 6: Disillusionment

Explain why you as a group think that this factor may prevent or discourage a person from exploring the key questions of life. Using various resources such as magazines, newspapers, statistics office, Internet, etc., find examples of this 'obstacle' in contemporary society. Your work should include evidence of the problems that can emerge when the search for meaning is hindered or blocked.

2. Choose a random selection of television advertisements. In groups, answer the following questions.

This topic is also considered in **Section B, Christianity: Origins and Contemporary Expression** and **Section I, Religion: The Irish Experience**.

- Describe in detail how each product is advertised.
- What image is associated with each product?
- What feeling is associated with each product?
- What is promised to the consumer if they buy the product being advertised?
- Are you convinced that the product being advertised can deliver on its promises? Explain.
- Can you think of other advertisements which promise the consumer happiness? Give examples.
- Why are young people persuaded by advertising?

Resources for further study
See teacher's text on CD-Rom for further suggestions.

Oral/Written Revision of Important Terms

Look up the following terms which you have come across in this chapter and briefly explain each one: **Culture, Generation X**, Maslow's '**hierarchy of needs**', **Consumerism**. Each term is printed in bold in the text.

Chapter 2: The Tradition of Search

He who cannot
draw on three
thousand years
is living from
hand to mouth.

(Goethe)

The Nature and Development of Philosophy

You will learn about...
- what philosophy is
- where it began
- who the first philosophers were
- the different aspects of philosophy

It is difficult for us to imagine that there was a time in human history when people did not think about being human and existing in the world. In fact, the ability to think about life in this way began in the sixth century before the Christian era. Before this time people had a mythical understanding of the world. They did not have scientific knowledge and so they formulated **myths** or stories that 'explained' life in a way that reflected their understanding. Each culture had its own myths which 'explained' how things came to be as they were. This mythical understanding was challenged by people called philosophers.

Philosophy means the 'love of wisdom', and all philosophy begins in wonder.

> 'Wonder is the feeling of a philosopher and philosophy begins in wonder.' (Plato)
> 'It is owing to their wonder that [people] both now begin and at the first began to philosophise.' (Aristotle)
> '...the only thing we require to be good philosophers is the faculty of wonder...'(Jostein Gaarder)

Consider

Put up the sheets of paper containing the key questions/issues suggested by students for the exercise on page 12. Comment on or add to these questions. Which question do you think is the most important and why? Can you suggest an 'answer' to this question? Have any of these questions come up in your life? How?

Read the following extract from the novel *Sophie's World* by Jostein Gaarder. In this novel a young girl begins a mysterious correspondence course in which she learns about philosophy. In one of the very early letters that she receives, her teacher tries to explain philosophy.

A lot of age-old enigmas have now been explained by science. What the dark side of the moon looks like was once shrouded in mystery. It was not the kind of thing that could be solved by discussion, it was left to the imagination of the individual. But today we know exactly what the dark side of the moon looks like, and no one can 'believe' any longer in the Man in the Moon, or that the moon is made out of green cheese.

A Greek philosopher who lived more that two thousand years ago believed that philosophy had its origin in man's sense of wonder. Man thought it was so astonishing to be alive that philosophical questions arose of their own accord.

It is like watching a magic trick. We cannot understand how it is done. So we ask: how can the magician change a couple of silk scarves into a live rabbit?

A lot of people experience the world with the same incredulity as when a magician suddenly pulls a rabbit out of a hat which has just been shown to be empty.

In the case of the rabbit, we know the magician has tricked us. What we would like to know is just how he did it. But when it comes to the world it is somewhat different. We know that the world is not all sleight of hand and deception because here we are in it, we are part of it. Actually, we are the white rabbit being pulled out of the hat. The only difference between us and the white rabbit is that the rabbit does not realise it is taking part in a magic trick. Unlike us. We feel we are a part of something mysterious and we would like to know how it all works.

P.S. As far as the white rabbit is concerned, it might be better to compare it with the whole universe. We who live here are microscopic insects existing deep down in the rabbit's fur. But philosophers are always trying to climb up the fine hairs of the fur in order to stare right into the magician's eyes.

Are you still there, Sophie? To be continued...[7]

The idea of the magician and the rabbit might be a helpful way for us to understand the nature of philosophy. It is about wonder and curiosity. At a particular time in our history, some people began to ask the kind of questions that became known as philosophical questions.

The natural philosophers

Human beings have always wondered about the nature of the universe and our place in it. But in Greece in the fifth and sixth centuries BCE, men like Thales, Anaximenes, Hereclitus and Parmenides began to develop a rational understanding of reality as opposed to a mythical understanding of reality. (We will be looking at the mythical understanding of reality later in chapter 5.)

In the Eastern Mediterranean, in places like Ionia, Greece and Asia Minor, human beings gradually became aware of the big questions of life and they began to reflect on this awareness. Philosophers began to ask questions regarding our true nature as human beings: how we know what we know, how we should behave, and the nature of the universe. Different philosophers explored these questions in different ways. Thales, Anaximenes and Hereclitus were concerned with the origin of things, and each one of them came up with a different theory. Thales believed that everything originated from water. Anaximenes believed that everything came from air. Hereclitus believed that fire was the source of everything. Parmenides and Hereclitus were particularly interested in understanding change and permanence, how things can change and yet remain themselves. These philosophers are known as the **natural philosophers** because they were concerned with the natural world. They are also known as the **pre-Socratic** philosophers because they came before one of the most important philosophers, Socrates.

Philosophy can be broken up into five distinct disciplines:

Metaphysics:
the study of being and the universe
Logic:
the study of reasoning
Ethics:
the study of moral behaviour
Anthropology:
the study of human nature
Epistemology:
the study of knowledge

For example, metaphysics examines the idea of existence by asking such questions as: what does it mean to be? to exist? to be real? We can see that philosophy is the process of asking such questions. Many people believe that all human beings, whether consciously or unconsciously, philosophise or have a philosophy of life. Philosophy strives to make clear through rational thought the nature of the universe and the nature and meaning of existence. Socrates, one of the greatest of all philosophers, claimed: 'The unexamined life is not worth living.'

It is with this belief that reflective people and reflective societies encourage critical and rational thinking about the meaning and purpose of life.

In summary

● Philosophy means the love of wisdom.

● All philosophy begins in wonder.

● Philosophy began in Greece in the fifth and sixth centuries BCE.

● The 'natural philosophers' were concerned with the natural world.

Class Debate

Prepare a class debate on the motion 'The unexamined life is not worth living'. Divide into two teams – for and against. Those not debating could act as researchers and debate officials. Perhaps you could invite other classes to attend the debate.

Questions

1. What is philosophy?
2. When did human beings begin to ask philosophical questions?
3. Where were the questions of human existence first asked?
4. What are the five disciplines of philosophy and what aspect of living does each one explore?
5. Who were the natural philosophers? Why were they given this name?

The Sophists

The fifth and sixth centuries BCE were a time of enormous political success for the Greeks. In 490 and again in 480 they defeated the Persians. This political and material success resulted in a flourishing of artistic creativity, as well as significant developments in the area of philosophy. From this period on Athens became the cultural centre of the Greek world and philosophy took a new direction. A group of thinkers emerged at this time, known as **the sophists.** They were educated men who travelled from place to place, offering tuition on subjects such as grammar, rhetoric and literature, as well as statesmanship and generalship. The emerging democracy in Athens required educated people. The sophists charged for their services, and so they were often employed by the wealthy and powerful. Those with money wanted to provide their children with professional training in the skills that would secure them successful careers, such as in the area of law and politics. The skills of rhetoric (debating, argument and application of logic) and persuasion were, therefore, much in demand.

Protagoras was one of the first of these professional teachers. He was born in Thrace in 480 BCE. The pre-Socratic philosophers or natural philosophers claimed to have discovered the truth about the origins of things; however, they all differed about the nature of this truth. The sophists were not concerned with the questions of the natural world, such as how the earth began; they were more concerned with the person and the person's place in the world. Protagoras came to the conclusion that it was not possible to know absolute truth. He believed that truth was a matter for each individual and that what is true for me may not be true for you but both positions are valid.

Protagoras said, 'Man is the measure of all things.'

This view led to the belief that the difference between good and evil cannot be known; no more than what is just and unjust. The sophists believed that other concepts of truth and justice were mere products of habit and circumstance, often created by those in power to suit their own interests. In the words of another sophist, Thrasymachus, 'Justice is simply the interest of the stronger.'

The sophists appealed to the politically ambitious younger generation because they could teach the skill of persuasion through **rhetoric**. They also developed the skills of debating and public-speaking. Students were

Questions

1. Who were the sophists?
2. Does 'sophistry' exist today and where is one likely to encounter it?
3. Is justice 'simply the interest of the stronger', as proclaimed by the sophists?

This topic is also considered in **Section D, Moral Decision-Making**.

Assignment

Write a brief note on the sophists and their role in the society of ancient Greece. Outline their importance in the development of philosophical thought.

taught to argue both sides of an issue with equal conviction, despite their own view. Truth itself was not the most important issue but rather the ability to persuade your audience of the truth of your position. The philosophy of the sophists created bitter disagreements in Athens because of their suggestion that there were no absolute norms for what was right and wrong. They contributed to a breakdown of the moral order; the lines of distinction between good and evil were no longer clear, and this caused problems in Greek society. The philosophers who followed, especially Socrates, Plato and Aristotle, disagreed with the views held by the sophists. We will now examine the work of these three men, who are considered to be three of the great philosophers because in their time they asked questions that had never previously been asked. They each offered important theories on ways of understanding the meaning of life and of human values.

In summary

- The sophists were a group of travelling philosophers.
- They lived in Athens during the fifth and sixth centuries BCE.
- They believed that there was no such thing as absolute good or evil, wrong or right; it all depended on the circumstances.

Socrates (470–399 BCE)

You will learn about...

- who Socrates was
- some of the central ideas in his philosophy

Socrates was born around 470 BCE. He lived in Athens during the height of its civilisation. He saw that Athens was in danger of destruction and so he became critical of the government. For this he was executed in 399. Socrates, we are told, was quite an intriguing character, whose appearance was the source of great comment in Athens; he is described as a strikingly ugly man who often travelled barefoot and is said to have worn the same garment winter and summer. The playwright Aristophanes referred to him as 'strutting like a waterfowl'. He seems to have been a man of great discipline who lived a virtuous life. He was an excellent soldier and exhibited great powers of strength and endurance. As a philosopher, Socrates was concerned with the question of **ethics**. He believed that it is the duty of the human person to explore the truth regarding right and wrong, justice and injustice, and courage and cowardice. Socrates wanted to establish a universal definition of justice. He worked to find certain laws and limits that could be observed in order to lead a good life. He believed that once you found these laws they would be

universal; that is, they would hold true for all peoples at all times and in all situations. In this he differed from the sophists, who believed in the **relativity** of moral issues; that is, that truth or justice depend on the situation or the context. Socrates felt that this position would lead to the destruction of the people of Athens.

Socrates' philosophy had a distinctive style. He engaged in a series of **dialogues** with people who believed they fully understood the issues under discussion. He would take the role of ignorant questioner and, through asking a few good questions, he would show the 'experts' how much they did not know. The aim of these philosophical dialogues was to discover the truth about how one should live a good and moral life. Socrates himself learned through this process and he also encouraged others to question their beliefs and knowledge.

Questions

1. Which philosophical discipline is associated with Socrates?
2. How did Socrates differ from the sophists on the question of justice and truth?
3. What was the purpose of life for Socrates?
4. How did Socrates use dialogue?
5. Socrates believed in the existence of a universal moral law. What does the word 'universal' mean?
6. Describe two ideas of Socrates.

In Socratic philosophy, the soul is very important. Socrates believed that the soul had to be cared for. He believed that the gaining of wisdom was the key to living a **virtuous** life and thereby saving the soul. For Socrates, knowing what was good was the same as doing what was good. Later philosophers disagreed with him on this point; they argued that a person might know what good is but might not be strong enough or disciplined enough to do the good. An example of Socrates' thinking can be found in his reflections on the use of alcohol. He believed that an action is right when it promotes humanity's true happiness; so, while it may be a pleasurable experience to get drunk constantly, especially if a person is unhappy with life, it is not conducive to the true good of humanity. Drunkenness will ultimately lead to ill health and can enslave a person in a habit; it goes against humanity's highest ability, which is the use of reason. Socrates believed pleasure to be good, but he held that true pleasure and lasting happiness were to be attained through moral living.

In summary

- Socrates was a philosopher in Athens in the sixth century BCE.
- He was concerned with the question of ethics: right and wrong, good and evil, justice and injustice. He moved philosophy beyond reflections on the natural world.
- Socrates believed that the soul had to be cared for, and this could be done by the gaining of wisdom – knowing what was good led to doing what was good.

Plato (428–347 BCE)

You will learn about...

- who Plato was and where he lived
- some of the central ideas of Plato's philosophy
- Plato's story of the Cave

Plato was born in Athens in 428 BCE to a prominent family. He considered a career in politics but rejected this, having become disillusioned by Athenian society and, most particularly, by the treatment and execution of Socrates. Plato was a devoted follower and friend of Socrates, having become his pupil when he was twenty. He left Athens for his own safety after the death of Socrates, and he travelled through Asia Minor, Egypt, Southern Italy and Greece before returning to Athens in 388. There he founded the Academy, which became the first European university and lasted until 529 CE. Plato died in 347 and was buried in the grounds of the Academy. Like

Socrates, Plato believed that true knowledge could be found only through the intellect, by reason, and not through the senses. He distrusted knowledge received through the senses because the material world is subject to change; things grow, change, move, grow old and decay. Plato believed that for something truly to exist, it must have some unchangeability in it. For example, the human body changes, therefore, according to Plato, it does not truly exist; unlike the soul, which is spiritual and does not change, therefore it exists. Plato, like Socrates, was concerned with how human beings should live (ethics). Both philosophers believed that humanity should be on a quest for good, for truth and for beauty. Plato believed that humanity should be on a journey 'upward' from the material to the spiritual. While Socrates remained very much within the philosophy of ethics, Plato went further than Socrates. Socrates asked questions like: what is justice? what is temperance? what is goodness? Plato sought to understand reality and how we perceive it. He began to ask questions like: what is roundness? what is treeness? what is blackness? In so doing, Plato began to be interested in the question of meaning and understanding, otherwise known as metaphysics.

Plato's concern for meaning, combined with his distrust of the senses, resulted in his theory of ideas. He believed that human beings are exposed to two worlds at once: on the one hand there is the world of the senses – this is a world of appearances and change; the other world is the truly authentic, unchanging world of the idea. In order to illustrate his theory Plato came up with an image, known as the Cave image, which he explained in his book, *The Republic*.

The story of the Cave

A tribe of people live chained in a dark cave. They face a blank wall, with a fire at their backs. In the light thrown by the fire, objects that pass in front of it create shadows on the wall. All the prisoners can see are the shadows moving across the wall. This is all they have ever seen since birth and so they understand this to be reality. They will only escape this life of illusion when they turn away from the wall and move out into the sunlight, the light of what is real. Eventually one prisoner escapes from the cave. At first he is confused and blinded by the light of the sun. However, when he adjusts he sees how perfect and bright are the real objects in comparison to the shadows that he thought were real.

What does he do? Does he go about his business enjoying his new found knowledge and understanding? No. This former prisoner returns to the cave to tell the others about the real world and to encourage them to recognise their world for what it is – illusion. The other prisoners do not welcome him. They see him as a threat and as someone who wants to upset their way of seeing things. They resist all attempts to change their position.

This story is an **allegory**, a teaching tool through which Plato outlines some of his beliefs. The world of ideas is the real world. The world we perceive through our senses is illusion. It is an imperfect shadow of the more perfect world we can come to understand using our mind. The philosopher, like the escaped prisoner, must teach others about the real world of ideas and help them to come into the light of true understanding.

Plato believed that everything perceived through the senses is merely appearance. True reality is the realm of ideas. The physical world is in a continual state of change, whereas the world perceived through the mind is unchanging and eternal. Each idea, for example blackness or treeness or roundness, offers a pattern for the physical object which is everchanging, while the idea remains unchanging. There are many trees that we can see, but they are only shadows or copies of the perfect idea of a tree that exists in another realm.

Sophie's World

In the novel *Sophie's World* by Jostein Gaarder, the little girl of the title gets to meet Plato and he asks her to think about four questions.

> My name is Plato and I am going to give you four tasks. First you must think over how a baker can bake fifty absolutely identical biscuits. Then you can ask yourself why all horses are the same. Next you must decide whether

1. Why did Plato become disillusioned?
2. Plato began to be interested in metaphysics. What do you understand by this?
3. What are the two worlds to which Plato believed human beings are exposed?
4. Which of the two worlds was the more highly valued by Plato? Explain your answer.

you think that [the human person] has an immortal soul. And finally you must say whether men and women are equally sensible. Good luck![8]

Now you have a go at answering these questions. Listen to what the other students in the class have to say about them. Remember, you are now doing philosophy!

Arising from Plato's distrust of the senses was an understanding of the human person as deeply divided. Plato saw the body and soul in conflict. In a sense, the body imprisoned the soul. This is known as a **dualistic understanding** of the human person, and this type of understanding has surfaced from time to time throughout the history of ideas.

In summary

- Plato was a student of Socrates. He founded his own school, called the Academy.
- Plato believed that true knowledge could only be found through the intellect, the mind. The senses could not be trusted.
- His theory of ideas stated that there are pure, unchangeable ideas which human beings may 'forget' but which can be understood through the use of the intellect.
- In his parable of the Cave, Plato explained his theory of ideas.

Aristotle (384–322 BCE)

You will learn about...

- who Aristotle was and where he lived
- the development of his thinking and teaching
- some of the central ideas in the philosophy of Aristotle

Aristotle was born in 384 BCE at Stageira in Thrace. He was a son of a physician of the Macedonian king Amyntas II. When he was seventeen he went to study in Plato's Academy in Athens. He remained there for over twenty years, as both a pupil and a teacher. He was a devoted pupil and friend of Plato. In later years, after Plato's death, Aristotle's teaching went in a different direction. He continued to be influenced by the teachings of Plato but his thought became more scientific as he grew older. This means that he became interested in proof and the principle of cause and effect in his arguments. He left Athens and spent three years tutoring the young Alexander the Great. In 335 he returned to Athens and founded his own school, called the Lyceum. He died in 322.

The writings of Aristotle can be divided into three main periods:

- ● **The period of his time with Plato**
- ● **The period spent at Assos and Mitylene**
- ● **The period of his leadership of the Lyceum in Athens**

In his early period Aristotle believed, as did Plato, that 'Life apart from the body is the soul's normal state'. In his second period he began to move away from his previously held **Platonic** beliefs. He became more critical of the teaching of the Academy, particularly Plato's theory of ideas. In his third period Aristotle became interested in the **empirical** (based on experience) and **scientific** aspects of life.

Form and matter

Like Plato, Aristotle believed that there was only one 'whiteness', 'treeness', 'justice', etc. They both believed that, for example, 'whiteness' is in all white things, 'treeness' in all trees, 'justice' in all just acts.

Plato called these 'ideas'. Aristotle renamed them 'forms'. Aristotle went on to develop a theory of form and matter that recognised both the essence of something and its physical manifestation and limitation, that is, what makes something unique and the physical characteristics it exhibits. All things in the world are made up of two principles – the form and the matter. The **form** is that which makes something what it is, for example its 'treeness', its 'manness'. However, form alone is not enough; 'manness' or 'treeness' cannot exist themselves; there must be another aspect that ties these forms down to a particular time and place, for example, a particular man or tree. This second principle, which makes the thing individual and concrete, is what Aristotle calls **matter**. This belief in the two basic principles of form and matter was a significant development in philosophical thought. From Aristotle's teaching there came the understanding that there is a part of everything that stays the same and there is a part of everything that changes. For example, all trees share something we can call 'treeness', but each tree is individual and changes according to circumstances. For Aristotle, form cannot exist without matter, neither can matter exist without form. The idea of a tree makes no sense without the bark, leaves and trunk. The fact that form and matter are equally important marks a development from Plato's more dualistic understanding of being, where physical things were in conflict with that which was considered superior, the spiritual.

Aristotle made an important contribution to the development of scientific thinking and principles. He believed that our knowledge begins with the senses; that is, what we see and hear, etc. We then move from the particular experience to the general. An example of this would be the use of a particular medicine. A person may know that a certain medicine cured him when he had a particular illness, but he may have no idea why. A more enlightened person may know the reason why it cured him; he knows that he was suffering from a fever and this particular medicine has a certain property that brings down a fever. This person now has what Aristotle calls a 'universal' because he knows that the medicine will tend to cure all those who suffer from fever.[9] According to Aristotle, we have two ways of knowing – through the senses initially and then through the intellect. They should be used in cooperation for total understanding of the world. Aristotle seems to be the philosopher who discovered that not only must we use our eyes and ears, but we must use our heads too! Through our senses we learn about the changing aspects of things, and through our intellect we understand the things that remain unchanging. For example, we can see the changes in the seasons: the leaves fall from the trees; the earth grows cold and animals hibernate. However, our intellect tells us that spring will come, leaves will grow and the earth will wake up. This understanding that in the midst of change there is stability allowed Aristotle to lay the foundations for scientific thought and principles.

You have scientific knowledge when you can explain why something happens. Common sense can tell us that water

Questions

1. Who was Alexander the Great?
2. What was the Lyceum?
3. What did Aristotle mean by (i) form, (ii) matter?
4. According to Aristotle, what are the two ways of knowing?
5. How did the thinking of Aristotle lay the foundations for scientific thought and principles?
6. How does Aristotle's thinking differ from that of Plato?

expanding into steam will exert pressure; scientific knowledge tells us why and can predict with certainty the degree of pressure that a given amount of steam will exert on a measured surface.[10]

In summary

- Aristotle moved beyond Plato in his recognition that we know the world through the senses.
- He believed in the principles of form and matter. Everything has both form and matter, and both are equally important.
- Aristotle is recognised for his contribution to scientific thought and principles.

FROM CLASSICAL TO CONTEMPORARY

You will learn about...

- three key moments in the development of philosophical thought
- some philosophers from each of these moments.

While the search for meaning continued, the direction of this search changed and developed through the centuries. We will look at three important developments that took place between classical times (the time of the Greek philosophers) and the contemporary period.

Christian Philosophers

You will learn about...

- Augustine and his beliefs
- Thomas Aquinas and his beliefs

The emergence of Christian philosophers in the late classical and medieval world was important. Augustine and Aquinas were two of the great Christian philosophers. While eight centuries separate these men, they both worked to bridge the thought of the Greek philosophers with the Christian faith.

Augustine of Hippo

Augustine of Hippo (354-430 CE) was born in Tagaste near Carthage (modern-day Tunisia). He converted to Christianity in 387 and became a bishop in 395. As a young man Augustine came under the influence of a sect called **Manichaeism**, which was similar to astrology in that it had a **determinist** view of the world; that is, a belief that our futures are mapped out for us. This group also had a deeply materialistic view of the world. Augustine rejected Manichaeism for a more spiritual understanding of life. He also came to believe that human beings have free will

and, therefore, the power to influence what happens in their lives. Augustine's beliefs were influenced by his Christian faith and by the teachings of Plato and his followers. In his most famous work, The Confessions, he outlines his belief that all humans are on a journey in search of happiness. Augustine's Christian faith convinced him that true happiness was only to be found in the Lord: 'You have made us for yourself O Lord and our hearts are restless until they rest in you' (Confessions 1:1).

Augustine recognised that not all human beings engaged in the search for meaning. He believed that the inability to search stemmed from a mistaken belief in one's own self-sufficiency; people like this were either in despair and could not believe in the possibility of happiness, or their lives were shaped by pride and this convinced them that they did not need God. Augustine believed that the human person desires above all else to love and be loved. He was convinced of the importance of searching for the truth, and he regarded truth as a gift from God. He believed that it is God who seeks us and offers us his love; we, in turn, through the experience of being loved, are able to love. The importance of friendship and love cannot be overstated in the philosophy of Augustine. Friendship and love were also very important to Plato. However, Augustine's understanding went beyond the Greek ideal. For the Greek philosophers, friendship and love were founded on the experience of attractiveness or sharing a common understanding of virtue. For Augustine as a Christian philosopher, the concept of love included love of enemies. 'It is the love of enemies that is the touchstone of a love that is "In God".'[1]

Thomas Aquinas

Aquinas was born in 1225 CE in the Italian town of Aquino. He studied and lectured in Paris and was a member of the Dominican Order. He is considered to be one of the greatest Christian philosophers and theologians of all time. His most famous work is the Summa Theologica. Aquinas died in 1274. Augustine was

Questions

1. Why do we refer to Augustine and Aquinas as two of the great Christian philosophers?

2. What did Augustine believe the human person desired above all else?

3. 'Properly human action is action that pursues goals' – What do you understand by this statement of Aquinas?

4. What, according to Aquinas, is the ultimate goal of life?

5. Who were the main philosophical influences on Augustine and Aquinas?

Assignments

1. Describe Augustine's concept of love.

2. Write a brief note on Manichaeism and Augustine's reaction to it.

influenced by the work of Plato and the **Neoplatonists** in his development of a Christian philosophy. Aquinas, on the other hand, used the philosophy of Aristotle in his work. Aquinas, like Augustine, was concerned with the question of human happiness and he also wrote about friendship and love. Aquinas believed that all nature pursues goals. He believed that this was particularly true for humans: 'Properly human action is action that pursues goals' (*Summa Theologica*, 1.2.1:1).

A simple thing such as movement is dependent on a goal; for example, one has a reason to move in one direction rather than another. He believed that the goal or reason for an action tells us whether it is good or bad.

Aquinas extended this thinking to the notion that we all have an ultimate goal. For Aquinas, this ultimate goal is God. He did recognise that not all people agreed on this point: 'So all [people] agree in pursuing an ultimate goal and seeking their own fulfilment, but they disagree as to where this fulfilment can be found; just as all [people] like their food tasty, yet disagree as to which food is the tastiest...(even) sinners turn away from the true ultimate goal, but not from an ultimate goal as such, since that is what they seek falsely in other things' (*Summa Theologica*, 1.2.1:7).

Aquinas asked whether happiness was to be found in riches and honours and fame, in power, in pleasure; his conclusion was 'no'. He believed that only God, the complete good, can satisfy the human desire for happiness. Like Aristotle, Aquinas believed that only those who live a virtuous life and seek the good will achieve happiness.

In summary

● Augustine and Aquinas were two of the great Christian philosophers.

● Augustine lived in the fourth century CE. He was a man of faith, influenced by the teachings of Plato.

● Augustine's most famous work was *The Confessions*. His philosophy expressed his belief that human beings have free will and that human beings desire to love and be loved above all else.

● Aquinas lived in the thirteenth century in Italy. He was a man of faith, influenced by the teachings of Aristotle.

● Aquinas's most famous work was the *Summa Theologica*. He believed that all of nature pursues goals and the ultimate goal is God.

The Age of Reason

You will learn about...

- when the Age of Reason happened
- what events influenced people to engage in a new way of thinking
- René Descartes and his beliefs

The Age of Reason, also called the **Enlightenment**, marked a significant point in human history. The seventeenth and eighteenth centuries were times of great development and change in the areas of scientific knowledge, geographical exploration and religious belief and attitudes. It is not surprising to learn that tension and conflict grew between the worlds of science and religion, sometimes caused by a misunderstanding of both. Scientists like Copernicus, Galileo and Newton were posing scientific theories that seemed to challenge the Church's understanding of the universe and its interpretation of the Bible. In 1610 Galileo came to prominence when, following Copernicus, he asserted that the earth moved around the sun rather than the other way round as people had believed up to then. In the Old Testament Joshua 10:13 stated:

> And the sun stood still, and the moon stopped,
> until the nation took vengeance on their enemies.
> Is this not written in the Book of Jashar? The sun stopped in
> midheaven, and did not hurry to set for about a whole day.

The Church condemned Galileo and ordered him to recant. This demonstrated an inadequate grasp of the nature of science by the Church of the time and also a literal understanding of biblical interpretation which we would not hold today. Pope John Paul II acknowledged this when he apologised in 1992 for the treatment of Galileo. Enlightenment thinkers proposed a view of the human person and human nature that suggested that people were responsible for their own destiny and did not need God or the Church to show them how to live their lives. Inevitably conflict ensued. Enlightenment thinkers sometimes displayed an exaggerated confidence in people's abilities to manage their own affairs; the Church sometimes did not fully acknowledge the role of personal responsibility and free will. Many philosophers were also Christians and they did not wish to diminish their faith in God. They worked very hard to reconcile the place of religious belief in a world where science and rational thought were to the forefront. We will examine the work of one of these men.

René Descartes (1596-1650)

Descartes was born in 1596 in a small town in Tours in France. He was the son of a landowner and councillor of the parliament of

RENE DES CARTES

Brittany. Having studied in the Jesuit college of Le Fleche in Anjou, Descartes travelled through Europe. It was while on this journey that he decided to delve more deeply into the philosophical questions of life. He was particularly interested in the question of human existence.

Metaphysics

    Descartes is often called the father of modern philosophy. He developed the first and most systematic philosophy based on an understanding of the human person as a rational and **autonomous** being. This was in opposition to the view of the person as entirely at the mercy of divine authority. However, Descartes believed in the existence of God, and this belief came from his rational reflections on human existence. Descartes' educational background was rooted firmly in the philosophy of Aristotle. Aristotle placed great significance on the authority of tradition and of the senses. Descartes rejected these fundamental elements of ancient

1. What do you understand by the Enlightenment?
2. Why is Descartes often called the father of modern philosophy?
3. What was Descartes' understanding of the human person?
4. What fundamental elements of ancient philosophy did Descartes reject?
5. What was the starting place for philosophy in Descartes' view?

Assignment

Briefly explain Descartes' 'Cogito argument' and its importance in the development of philosophical thought.

This topic is also considered in **Section J, Religion and Science** and **Section I, Religion: the Irish Experience**.

philosophy and, in so doing, gave life to modern philosophy. He began from a position of doubt. He doubted almost all knowledge acquired through the senses and from other people. His philosophy demanded that we question all the beliefs and assumptions that we have picked up along life's journey. He believed that to gain truth we must reject all the prejudices and beliefs learned through the senses. For Descartes, the self is the starting place of knowledge.

The discovery of the existence of self is the point of certainty; 'I think therefore I am'. It is from here that all meaningful reflection must come. This belief has come to be known as the **'Cogito argument'**. From this premise Descartes created his philosophical system. He believed that it is the intellect that tells me that 'I think therefore I am', and as such, in Descartes' view, it is far more reliable than knowledge gained from the senses. Descartes wanted to develop his philosophy, beginning with himself and his God-given ability to reason. He believed that knowledge begins in metaphysics (the study of being and the universe), and metaphysics begins with the self, and from the self we arrive at God. The importance of the 'I' or the 'self' in the philosophy of Descartes is known as the turn to the subject.

In *Sophie's World*, Sophie and her mentor discuss Descartes:

The idea of a perfect entity cannot have originated from one who was himself imperfect, he claimed. Therefore the idea of a perfect entity must have originated from that perfect entity itself, or in other words, from God. That God exists was therefore just as self-evident for Descartes as that a thinking being must exist.

Now he was jumping to a conclusion. He was more cautious to begin with.[12]

In summary

● The Age of Reason refers to a period in the seventeenth and eighteenth centuries in Europe.

● Advancements in scientific thought challenged traditional beliefs in God.

● René Descartes lived in France in the seventeenth century. He was influenced by the teachings of Aristotle and the scientific advances of his time.

● Descartes distrusted knowledge gained through the senses and concluded that knowledge is to be found through our God-given ability to reason.

● Descartes believed that the person is a rational, autonomous being. This is summed up in his statement, 'I think therefore I am'

Romanticism and Existentialism

You will learn about...

- the age of romanticism and existentialism
- what the Romantics believed and how they differed from the thinkers of the Enlightenment
- the central beliefs of the existentialists
- Friedrich Nietzsche and his beliefs

The eighteenth and nineteenth centuries saw a new era in philosophical thought and indeed in the world of art and literature. **Romanticism** was a movement that developed in reaction to the Age of Enlightenment, where reason was highly valued. This movement is not easy to categorise, but in literature and philosophy it expressed a new celebration of human passion. The Enlightenment thinkers believed that reason existed in order to control the senses. For them, the human ability to rationalise was what distinguished humans from animals. It was only through the use of reason and the intellect that human beings could control their sensual natures and thereby attain justice and truth. The Romantics disagreed. They believed that the emotions experienced by humans were not separate from reason and the intellect. Both aspects of the human person were valued and integrated in order to ensure that creativity and individuality is preserved. The Romantics believed that reliance on reason alone threatened to stifle the creative aspects of the human person. The philosophical school of thought known as **existentialism** emerged from this reaction to the Enlightenment. A Danish man named Soren Kierkegaard was the first philosopher to be called an existentialist. For the existentialists, the formation of human identity was of the utmost importance. Human autonomy (independence) and free will were the hallmarks of existentialist thinking. The influence of society on the identity of the individual meant that it was difficult to become truly independent. We will now explore the philosophy of Friedrich Nietzsche.

Friedrich Nietzsche (1844-1890)

Nietzsche was born in Prussia in 1844. He was the son of a Protestant pastor. A brilliant student, he was awarded a professorship of classical philosophy at the University of Basel at the age of twenty-five, before he had completed his doctorate. Nietzsche suffered ill health for most of his life and he had to resign from his position in the University of Basel in 1879. For the next ten years he lived in many different places and wrote extensively. However, his mental health deteriorated and he died in 1890. Nietzsche could be described as one of the most notorious philosophers that we will study. His ideas were controversial at the time he was writing and they have had an enormous influence on modern philosophy. Nietzsche's philosophy emerged from his **scepticism**; that is to say, he believed that there was no absolute, moral or scientific truth. For Nietzsche, the concept of truth is merely something that society needs in order to control its people and function efficiently. A consequence of Nietzsche's theory that an absolute moral truth does not exist is that there cannot then be an absolute notion of good and evil. This, as you can imagine, went contrary to the beliefs of many people at the time. It particularly offended Christians, whose belief in moral truth was central to the teachings of the Church. Nietzsche accused Christianity of producing what he called a 'slave morality'. According to Nietzsche, human behaviour should be judged in terms of greatness and excellence. The power of the will becomes very important in Nietzsche's view of the person. Those who achieve greatness or excellence at leadership or in other areas of life will be judged successful.

One of Nietzsche's most infamous pronouncements was that 'God is dead'. The values and morality of European culture grew out of belief in God. Nietzsche believed that faith in God was no longer credible in a world where most things could be explained without reference to a higher being; it was human beings, through their use of reason, who had made belief in God incredible and, therefore, the morality based on this belief was no longer applicable. This led Nietzsche to conclude that the old moral order would collapse, giving rise to a new philosophy of extreme scepticism, called nihilism.

Questions

1. How and why did the age of romanticism develop in the eighteenth century?
2. What is the starting point of Nietzsche's philosophy?
3. What was Nietzsche's theory about good and evil?
4. Explain nihilism in your own words.
5. What did Nietzsche mean by 'God is dead'?

In summary

● The age of romanticism and existentialism belongs to the eighteenth and nineteenth centuries.

● The Romantics believed that the emotions were as important as the intellect for human growth and development.

● The existentialists believed that the formation of identity was extremely important. Independence and free will were central to their philosophy.

● Friedrich Nietzsche lived in Prussia in the nineteenth century. He believed there was no absolute moral or scientific truth. For Nietzsche, truth was a human invention, designed to keep order and control.

● In Nietzsche's philosophy, human behaviour should be judged in terms of greatness and excellence. The power of the will is important.

Assignment

Write a short note on each of the three key moments in philosophical thought from classical to contemporary times. Refer to one key philosopher from each period and mention their contribution to philosophy.

Oral/Written Revision of Important Terms

Look up the following terms which you have come across in **bold** type in this chapter and briefly explain each one: **myth, philosophy, natural philosophers, pre-Socratic, the sophists, rhetoric, ethics, relativity, dialogues of Socrates, virtuous, allegory, dualistic understanding, Platonic, empirical approach, scientific approach, form and matter, Manichaeism, determinist, Neoplatonists, Enlightenment, autonomous, 'Cogito argument', romanticism, existentialism, scepticism.**

Part Two: The Response to the Quest

Chapter 3: The Language of Symbol

He has made
everything
suitable for its
time; moreover,
he has put a
sense of past
and future into
their minds, yet
they cannot find
out what God
has done from
the beginning to
the end.

(Book of Ecclesiastes 3:11)

In this chapter you will learn about...

● symbol; what it is and how it emerged in the human response to the search for meaning and values

● the power of symbol on individuals, groups and societies

● the relationship between symbol and ritual

It is in our nature as human beings to want to know 'why' and to look for meaning in the world around us. We need a reason for everything, particularly life, death, suffering, happiness and other such important realities. These represent what we consider to be the great questions of life: why do people suffer? why should death come to one so young? what is the secret of happiness? why me?

These questions are not alone familiar to all human beings, but resonate in the depths of their being. Religion asks these questions from a particular perspective. All religions assume that the world is meaningful. Religion assumes and believes in a 'creator' which gives meaning to the created. At the heart of all religion is the sense that there is meaning to our world and possibly answers to the great questions of life. Religion recognises the existence of more than we can name – something 'other' than that which we can see or touch. Religion calls this 'otherness' the **sacred**.

Do the following exercises and share your responses with your group.

1. Identify three objects that are important to you. They may be a card, a book, a song or piece of music, an item of jewellery, a photograph, a letter … anything that means a lot to you.
   List the three items and say why each is important. Where do you keep this object? When do you look at it/ listen to it, etc? What do each of these objects symbolise for you?

2. Think of any other symbols in our modern culture, for example a symbol of Ireland, Europe, Love, Africa, Wealth, Christianity, Islam, Ecology, Peace, etc. Discuss the meanings behind these symbols.

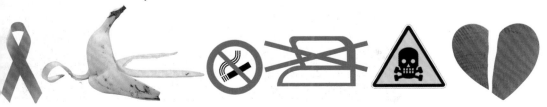

When Words Are Not Enough

In our struggle to understand the great questions of life we create **symbols**. Because the great questions of life are usually concerned with abstract things like love, death, suffering, happiness, etc., we find it difficult to express our hopes, fears and expectations using words alone. Some of our most profound experiences in life can leave us speechless or at least struggling to express ourselves. Sometimes words alone are not enough and sometimes we need to use words in a different way in order to touch upon the greater mysteries of life. We struggle to name realities and experiences, and in doing so we create symbols. We respond symbolically to the great mysteries of life. The creation and use of symbols is a distinctively human phenomenon.

We attach meaning to objects, words, music, colour, etc. when we need to say something or acknowledge something that is bigger than ourselves. Symbols are our effort to name and *participate in* what is abstract or 'other'. For example, married love is symbolised by a ring, peace is symbolised by a white dove, the cross is a symbol of sacrifice, suffering or love of Christ, depending on when and how it is used. A hug is a symbol that works between two individuals. It is a personal expression of affection or forgiveness or sorrow. It is important to distinguish between sign and symbol. A sign is a straightforward, uncomplicated thing, like a traffic sign or a sign indicating a direction. There are no nuances and almost always only one clear meaning attached to a sign. A symbol, in contrast, is a complex, multifaceted entity that can have many meanings depending on the context. For example, the symbols of a closed fist, human tears, a bunch of flowers may have many levels of meaning depending on where, when, how and by whom they are used. New meaning can be added if necessary.

Symbols and Ritual

Symbols speak to us as individuals on many levels. We understand them on a deep level; this understanding is often instinctual. Symbols speak to our minds and to our hearts; they move us deeply and communicate meaning to us. The symbol of the cross or perhaps the symbol of a national flag speaks to groups of people gathered together. Such symbols indicate that the group is gathered together in common cause or origin. We engage with the great questions of life through symbols. Ritual is inextricably linked with symbol. **Ritual** is to symbol as dancer is to dance. Ritual is the repeated, commonly recognised behaviour through which a community engages with the mysteries of life. Through ritual, human beings mark key moments in the life of the individual and the community. Symbols are significant for society at a time of death or tragedy. Flowers left at the site of an accident, black ribbons on a doorway, the tolling of a bell are all symbols used in wider society to express compassion and grief. Perhaps these symbols allow people to express their solidarity with others. They can represent the society and, as such, are recognised by all.

Questions

. What is the difference between sign and symbol?
. Can you explain the concept of symbol?
. Why do humans create symbols?
. Give examples of symbols in your culture. How do they work?
. Can you describe a symbol that has personal significance for you?
. Identify two contemporary religious symbols.
. Identify and comment on symbols that are significant for individuals, groups and wider society.

Religious Symbols

When we as individuals, as a family, as a nation or as a culture endow something with meaning, and when it comes to represent something and be sacred, then it is a religious symbol. When an object, a gesture, music or words become symbols of the sacred, then they are religious symbols. Familiar religious symbols include the sign of the cross, a bowed head, joined hands, prayers, a crucifix, a rosary beads, vestments, chalice, incense, a tolling bell; the list could go on and on. Human beings have created religious symbols from almost the beginning of time. They have responded to the great questions of life: why are we here? why do we die? is death the end? why do people suffer? where did we come from? Symbol and ritual are the means through which humans have responded to these questions.

Clearly science has answered some of the questions that the earliest human beings asked, such as those concerning the nature and composition of the earth, the galaxies, the origins of life and the structure of early humans, to name but a few. However, some of the central questions remain in the hearts of people everywhere: why are we here? what is our purpose? why do bad things happen to some people? why is there suffering and pain? is death the end? does the human spirit live on? is there a God? are we responsible for the earth or for each other? is there meaning in the universe? These are religious questions. Each religion of the world approaches these questions from a particular perspective.

In summary

● Sometimes words are not adequate to express our human response to the search for meaning.

● Symbols are our effort to name and participate in what is abstract or other.

● Symbol and ritual are inextricably linked.

his topic is also onsidered in **Section G, Vorship, Prayer and itual** and **Section H, he Bible: Literature nd Sacred Text**.

Oral/Written Revision of Important Terms

Look up the following terms which you have come across in **bold** type in this chapter and briefly explain each one: **sacred, symbols, ritual.**

Chapter 4: The Tradition of Response

In this chapter you will learn about...

● myth and its role in the response of ancient peoples to the great questions of life

● the myth of Prometheus, the myth of Gilgamesh and the Native American creation myth

● early religious behaviour

● the sense of the sacred in contemporary culture

● the religious and non-religious responses to the search for meaning in contemporary culture

Symbolic Stories

One of earliest ways in which people communicated their understanding of the world and their place in it was through myths. A **myth** is a story created by ancient people which expresses their understanding of and beliefs about their world. These myths were explanations of why things were the way they were. They came before philosophy and science and as such represent the earliest evidence for humanity's search for meaning. As we have seen in chapter 2, philosophers later began to question this mythical understanding of reality and to apply reason and logic to such questions.

The following extract, based on the myth of Prometheus, tries to explain the origin of fire as well as the origin of old age, labour, sickness, insanity, vice and passion. According to the Greeks of the day, Prometheus was the creator of humanity. The myth tells of how Prometheus angered Zeus by being too powerful and clever. Zeus was the father of Heaven and the grandson of Mother Earth. He was the most powerful of gods and he controlled them all. In his anger at Prometheus, Zeus decided to withhold fire from humanity, so Prometheus sought another route to Olympus, the place of the gods, where he could obtain fire.

The myth of Prometheus
Zeus was the wisest of all the gods. He had grown angry with the whole of humanity and was about to destroy them but for the pleading of Prometheus.

Prometheus went to Athene, requesting a backstairs admittance to Olympus (the home of the gods), and this she granted. On arriving at Olympus, he lit a torch from the Sun and broke from it a piece of glowing charcoal. He threw it into a giant fennel-stalk, extinguished the torch and stole away undiscovered and gave fire to mankind.

Zeus was angry and swore revenge. He ordered Hephaestus to make a clay woman, and the four Winds to breathe life into her, and all the goddesses to adorn her. This woman was Pandora. She was the most beautiful woman ever created. She was offered to Epimetheus (Prometheus's brother) as a gift from Zeus, however he respectfully refused the gift, having been warned by his brother to accept no gift from Zeus. This made Zeus even angrier than before. Zeus had Prometheus chained naked to a pillar where a greedy vulture tore at his liver all day, and there was no end to the pain, because every night his liver grew whole again. But Zeus made excuses for his cruelty by saying that Athene had invited Prometheus to Olympus for a secret love affair.

Epimetheus, alarmed by his brother's fate, hastened to marry Pandora, whom Zeus had made as foolish, mischievous and idle as she was beautiful. Presently she opened a jar, which Prometheus had warned Epimetheus to keep closed, and in which he had been at pains to imprison all the Spites that might plague mankind: such as Old Age, Labour, Sickness, Insanity, Vice and Passion. Out these flew in a cloud, stung Epimetheus and Pandora, and then attacked the race of mortals. Delusive Hope, however, whom Prometheus had also shut in the jar, discouraged them by her lies from a general suicide.[13]

Questions

1. What is your understanding of myth?
2. What did the myth of Prometheus 'explain' for the people of the day?
3. In the light of this myth, what kind of god was Zeus?
4. How would you describe Pandora?
5. What was held in the jar opened by Pandora?
6. How did this myth help the people at the time in their search for meaning?

Myth and Early Cosmologies

We have evidence that the earliest societies sought to understand the **cosmos** – the order of the universe as a whole. The existence of ancient myths and cosmologies (theories about the nature of the universe) suggests a religious view of existence. Through myth and ritual early societies sought to give meaning and order – 'cosmos' – to the disorder and mystery – 'chaos' – that surrounded them. Bringing cosmos to chaos is part of being human. The word 'myth' comes from the Greek word *mythos*, meaning word or story. Stories are one of the means used by people to describe or explain things. Myths, particularly ancient myths, are stories created by ancient societies to explain the great mysteries of life.

These stories were passed from one generation to the next in the form of poetry, songs and legends. However, myths are more than stories: they deal with important realities like death, life, creation, beginning, ending, etc. Myths deal with abstract realities; some reveal to us how early societies understood the changing seasons, the sun, moon and stars, the origin of life and much more. World mythology can be classified into four key types of myth:

Cosmic myths:
Concerned with origins and order, these myths deal with the questions of existence and our place in the world. (Creation myths. etc.)

Theistic myths:
Concerned with gods/goddesses, the creator, the ultimate, and providers of meaning in the world. (Prometheus, Pan, etc.)

Hero myths:
Concerned with individuals and their journeys of discovery and revelation. (Odysseus, Cúchulainn, etc.)

Place/Object myths:
Concerned with particular places and/or objects of great significance. (King Arthur's sword, Newgrange, etc.)

The myth of Gilgamesh could be classified as both an object myth and a hero myth because it tells of a man called Gilgamesh and his journey to find the secret of eternal life. Gilgamesh was a legendary king who set out to find a potion that would guarantee immortality he wanted to bring this back to his people. The journey was fraught with difficulties and dangers.

The myth of Gilgamesh
After he had passed safely the lions that guard the foothills and the scorpion men who watch the heaven-supporting mountains, he came, amidst the mountains, to a paradise garden of flowers, fruits, and precious stones. Pressing on he arrived at the sea that surrounds the world. In a cave beside the waters dwelt a

manifestation of the goddess Ishtar...and this woman, closely veiled, closed the gate against him. But when he told her his tale, she admitted him to her presence and advised him not to pursue his quest, but to learn to be content with the mortal joys of life:

Cuneiform clay tablet with part of the Gilgamesh story, from the British Museum

Gilgamesh, why dost thou run about this way?
The life that thou art seeking, thou wilt never find.
When the gods created man,
they put death upon mankind,
and held life in their own hands.
Fill thy belly, Gilgamesh;
day and night enjoy thyself;
prepare each day some pleasant occasion.
Day and night be frolicsome and gay;
let thy clothes be handsome,
thy head shampooed, thy body bathed.
Regard the little one who takes thy hand.
Let thy wife be happy against thy bosom.

Comprehension

What advice does Ishtar give to Gilgamesh?

Gilgamesh insisted on carrying on with his journey. The goddess allowed him and warned him of the dangers on the way. Gilgamesh took a ferry across the waters of death, with the strict advice not to touch the waters. Upon reaching his destination he had to listen to a story of an ancient flood from the hero of that event, named Utnapishtim, who had instructions for Gilgamesh.

Then Utnapishtim bid his visitor sleep, and he slept for six days. Utnapishtim had his wife bake seven loaves and place them by the head of Gilgamesh as he lay asleep beside the boat. And Utnapishtim touched Gilgamesh, and he awoke, and the host ordered the ferryman Ursanapi to give the guest a bath in a certain pool and then fresh garments. Following that, Utnapishtim announced to Gilgamesh the secret of the plant.

Comprehension

What would happen if Gilgamesh kept the plant in his hand?

> Gilgamesh, something secret I will disclose to thee,
> and give thee thine instruction:
> That plant is like a brier in the field;
> its thorn, like that of the rose, will pierce thy hand.
> But if thy hand attain to that plant,
> thou wilt return to thy native land.

The plant was growing at the bottom of the cosmic sea. Ursanapi ferried the hero out again into the waters. Gilgamesh tied stones to his feet and plunged. Down he rushed, beyond every bound of endurance, while the ferryman remained in the boat. And when the diver had reached the bottom of the bottomless sea, he plucked the plant, though it mutilated his hand, cut off the stones, and made again for the surface. When he broke the surface and the ferryman had hauled him back into the boat, he announced his triumph:

Comprehension

What did Gilgamesh believe the plant would do for him?

> Ursanapi, this plant is the one...
> By which Man may attain full vigor.
> I will bring it back to Erech of the sheep-pens...
> Its name is: 'In his age, Man becomes young again.'
> I will eat of it and return to the condition of my youth.

Temple of the Sun-god, Babylon from the British Museum

Questions

1. What were the dangers Gilgamesh faced on his journey to find the secret of eternal life?
2. Who are the main characters of this myth?
3. What advice does the goddess give to Gilgamesh?
4. What mystery does this myth seek to address?
5. What natural phenomenon does the myth 'explain'?
6. Does this myth remind you of any other stories or myths?

They proceeded across the sea. When they had landed, Gilgamesh bathed in a cool water-hole and lay down to rest. But while he slept, a serpent smelled the wonderful perfume of the plant, darted forth, and carried it away. Eating it, the snake immediately gained the power of sloughing its skin, and so renewed its youth. But Gilgamesh, when he awoke, sat down and wept...[14]

The myths of any culture can be understood as the story of what that culture held to be sacred. The collection of myths contains the sacred narrative or story of the culture and as such it seeks to reveal the mystery of how things came to be.

Inca Temple, South America

In the mythologies of ancient cultures there are some universal elements, elements that are common to all cultures. In almost all of these mythologies there is the myth of the **sacred place.** Each culture sought to understand the relationship between the three levels of the world: the underworld, the earth and the heavens. A sacred place was created by symbolically bringing together these three levels. In some myths we find a reference to a sacred pillar or a pole. This 'cosmic pillar' can be found in myths across the world. In the world view of these traditional societies, a sacred place was a means of marking what was different and 'other'. This place usually had an opening through which one could pass from one level to another; this could be a doorway, a roof opening, a passageway, etc. In the sacred place the possibility of communicating with the heavens was symbolised by such things as a ladder, a pillar, a mountain, a tree, among others. Around this

49

sacred place was the rest of the world according to the ancient society. Thus this sacred place was the 'centre of the world'.[15] The motif of a sacred place, a city, a mountain, can be found in the mythologies of many different cultures. All of the world's major religions have this in their myths and rituals. This sacred place at the centre of the world is an expression of the connection between heaven and earth. Temples are human representations of the holy mountain.

In this Native American creation myth we can see how the Cherokee understood their world. We can also learn about the relationship between people and the natural world.

Native American creation myth

Long ago, before there were any people, the world was young and water covered everything. The earth was a great island floating above the seas, suspended by four rawhide ropes representing the four sacred directions. It hung down from the crystal sky. There were no people, but the animals lived in a home above the rainbow. Needing space, they sent Water Beetle to search for room under the seas. Water Beetle dove deep and brought up mud that spread quickly, turning into land that was flat and too soft and wet for the animals to live on. Grandfather Buzzard was sent to see if the land had hardened. When he flew over the earth, he found the mud had become solid; he flapped in for a closer look. The wind from his wings created valleys and mountains, and that is why the Cherokee territory has so many mountains today. As the earth stiffened, the animals came down from the rainbow. It was still dark. They needed light, so they pulled the sun out from behind the rainbow, but it was too bright and hot. A solution was urgently needed. The **shamans** were told to place the sun higher in the sky. A path was made for it to travel from east to west so that all the inhabitants could share in the light.

The plants were placed upon the earth. The Creator told the plants and animals to stay awake for seven days and seven nights. Only a few animals managed to do so, including the owls and mountain lions, and they were rewarded with the power to see in the dark. Among the plants, only the cedars, spruces, and pines remained awake. The Creator told these plants that they would keep their hair during the winter, while the other plants would lose theirs.

Questions

1. According to this creation myth, what was the first form of life on earth?
2. In what way might this be significant for a people?
3. How, according to the myth, were the mountains created?
4. In this creation story, why does the sun move from east to west?
5. How would you describe the Creator in this myth?
6. What does the myth reveal about the relationship between people and the earth?
7. Does this myth have anything to say to us today?

This topic is also considered in **Section G, Worship, Prayer and Ritual**.

People were created last. The women were able to have babies every seven days. They reproduced so quickly that the Creator feared the world would soon become too crowded. So after that the women could only have one child per year, and that is the way it has been ever since.[16]

Some myths reveal what ancient societies believed about how the world began, the existence of gods, the relationship of people to the earth and much more. In many cases modern humanity has a different understanding of these realities, yet they continue to be important concerns for people today. This search for answers is something that we share with our ancient ancestors. Myths contain information and insight about the nature of humanity, both in the past and in the present. They reveal to us how we as humans continue to struggle to find meaning and significance in our world. Myths are religious in nature in that they seek to give meaning to the 'other', the sacred in life. They are concerned with the great religious questions of life. Every great religion has its own collection of myths, which reveal how the followers understood life's great mysteries.

The Celtic world

Many of the ancient myths of the Celtic world explain some of the rituals still practised today. For example, the lighting of bonfires at Hallowe'en and the celebration of Hallowe'en itself have ancient mythic origins. The first of November was the date of the ancient pre-Christian festival of Samhain. This was a festival of the disappearing sun; the winter sun sinks lower in the sky as 21 December (shortest day and longest night) approaches. The people lit fires and said 'prayers' in order to ward off the darkness. The festival is also linked with the 'other' world, where the spirit of the dead rested. Samhain falls exactly halfway between the solstice on

Assignments

1. Give an account of a myth that attempted to address one of the great questions of life. In doing so, identify the ancient culture from which the myth originated and the question the myth sought to answer.
2. Write a note on the different types of myth created by ancient cultures.
3. Explain the significance of the concept of 'the sacred place' in all myths.
4. Write a note on the significance of the solstice in Irish mythology.

This topic is also considered in **Section I, Religion: the Irish Experience**.

21 September and the solstice on 21 December. This fact was not only deliberate but an intrinsic part of the festival. There were other major festivals linked to the solstices, three of which were successfully integrated into the Christian calendar after the arrival of Christianity to Ireland: Samhain became the feast of All Souls, followed by All Saints; Imbolg (1 February) became Saint Brigid's Day; Bealtaine (1 May) became dedicated to Mary. Only the festival of Lughnasa remained outside of Christian practice and effectively died out. Ireland is rich in archaeological evidence which points to early religions. Our literary culture and folk tales, even current religious practices, reveal a past rich in symbols, ritual and myth.

Early Religious Behaviour

Scholars generally agree that modern human beings came into existence approximately forty thousand years ago. The predecessors of 'Homo Sapiens' are estimated to have existed seventy thousand years ago! In the study of the past there are a few technical terms that would be helpful to understand.

Before the scientific discoveries of the most recent centuries, scholars sought to understand the origin of humanity; some scholars tried to put a date on the event. European scholars were influenced by the accepted belief of the time that the Bible was quite literally the word of God. Thus, they dated the origins of humanity based on the evidence in the Bible. However, other civilisations like the Greeks and the Egyptians believed that humankind was far more ancient than this. While we may stand in amazement at our ancestors' attempts to set such an exact date, it must be remembered that these people lived in a pre-scientific age, without the help of natural sciences or literary criticism. Archaeology today is about the study of the lives of ordinary people in the distant past – how they lived, what they ate, the tools they used and the rituals they practised. The study of the past has revealed much to us about the way our ancestors

1. When did Homo
   Sapiens come into
   existence, according
   to scholars?
2. What are the terms
   used to refer to the
   three Stone Ages?
3. What is meant by
   'religious' behaviour?
   Give examples of
   early religious
   behaviour.
4. 'Some European
   scholars completely
   miscalculated the
   date for the origins
   of humankind.'
   How and why did
   this occur?
5. Why were burial
   rituals so important
   for our forebears?

*Tollund Man,
believed to be two
thousand years old[17]*

**Resources for further
study**
See teacher's text on
CD-Rom for further
suggestions.

viewed themselves and their world. Evidence from the past is never complete. Archaeologists and historians evaluate the evidence and try to draw conclusions based on that evidence. Through archaeology and historical research we find much that suggests religious behaviour on the part of ancient peoples. By 'religious' we mean that they attached meaning to key moments in their lives, both as individuals and as a community. These significant times were marked in many ways, through ritual, through the building of structures or statues, through paintings and other artefacts. These rituals often coincided with a significant time of year. One set of rituals that are rich in information about how ancient societies sought meaning are the rituals of burial.

The burial of the dead[18]
Burial rituals by their very nature reveal much to us about how ancient societies viewed life, death and the question of an afterlife. Formal burial of the dead marks an important development in the history of ritual. Bodies were no longer simply abandoned or left to wild animals; instead, people sought to find meaning at this very difficult time. The drama of humanity is evident in the refusal to accept the brute fact of simply passing out of existence and in a deep desire to last beyond death. Archaeological excavations have revealed that ancient societies created rituals, sometimes very elaborate ones, around death and burial. There is rich evidence of ritual burial and/or cremation, of special clothing and ornamentation of the body, of special locations and structures for burial.

An example of an Irish megalithic tomb known as a dolmen

One of the many significant discoveries was made by Karl Maska in Moravia in 1984. Maska, an eminent Stone Age archaeologist, discovered a mass grave, approximately 25,000–30,000 years old, containing the remains of eighteen people – ten children and eight adults. The bodies were buried with ornaments and various other objects in a large oval pit covered with stone slabs and mammoth bones. No one knows whether these people were related or the significance of the mammoth bones. What is clear is that something significant was intended.

Evidence of a rich ritual life is also to be found in the later Neolithic settlement of Catal Hüyük in south central Turkey. This settlement is dated roughly between 6250 and 5400 BCE. During excavation it was discovered that the people of this settlement buried their dead beneath the floors of their houses. Individual families maintained their own burial site, which they opened when one of the family members died. What can we say about this practice? It is possible that the burial of the dead beneath a house that continued to be occupied indicated a belief that the dead were very much part of the living.

There is no doubt but that many ancient societies recognised death as an important event, a crossing between life and death. It is likely that death was an event surrounded by fear and wonder, a time when our ancient ancestors came close to one of the great mysteries of life.

Questions

1. Briefly describe burial rites from some ancient societies.
2. What does the ritual of burial tell us about ancient societies?
3. In what sense could these burial rituals be considered religious?

Rites of sacrifice

There is ample evidence to support the claim that ritual sacrifice was practised by some ancient societies. This involved giving something of value to the gods or god in order to show devotion or commitment.

In the religion of the ancient Israelites the sacrifice of an animal was carried out by ritual burning. Fire was a significant element of the ritual, symbolising the union between the person/group offering the sacrifice and the god.

Ritual sacrifice had several important functions in ancient societies. Sacrifice would have been offered in order to please the gods, perhaps to ensure the fertility of the soil for the next year's crops. Ancient peoples may also have offered sacrifice in thanksgiving for the first fruits of the harvest, in the belief that all life was the gift of the gods. Animal sacrifice was a common element of worship for the Israelites and this continued to be part of Jewish worship in the centuries before Christianity.

Aztec sacrificial altar

There is some evidence in history for the practice of human sacrifice, particularly at the burial of a king or great leader; attendants or soldiers were killed and buried with their leader, perhaps reflecting a belief that they would continue to serve their leader in the afterlife. A spectacular example of this practice was discovered in the 1920s–30s in ancient Mesopotamia (modern-day Iraq), where the archaeologist Sir Leonard Woolley uncovered tombs of Sumerian kings and queens, dating back to 5500 BCE. In one tomb there were remains of sixty-eight female and six male attendants, all richly adorned as befitting the attendants of a royal personage. In another tomb they found the remains of soldiers, with an ox cart and oxen guarding the entrance.

Perhaps a less ornate but no less dramatic example of human sacrifice was the discovery of the **Tollund Man** in 1960 in the Tollund Fen in Denmark. The preservative qualities of the peat bog in which the body was found played a significant part in the quality of this two thousand-year-old body. He was lying naked except for a cap and a belt. He lay as if sleeping, with his legs drawn up in a posture of calm repose. However, the presence of a rope around his neck indicated that he had been hung.

Many hundreds of bog people have been discovered over the years. The majority appear to have died violently by means such as hanging, blows to the head, stabbing, etc. Why? Perhaps they were criminals or in some way broke the rules of the society in which they lived. There is a strong suggestion that these people were ritually sacrificed, a theory supported by the discovery of vessels, ornaments and other artefacts at such sites.

Sacred art and artefacts

Sacred art and artefacts provide evidence from the ancient past. Historians and archaeologists examine these objects or paintings in an effort to understand ancient societies; they are like detectives looking for clues and answers. The human engagement with the great mysteries of life has given rise to some of the most beautiful and astonishing works of art. One example of the symbolic art through which ancient humans expressed their search for order within the cosmos can be found in Newgrange in County Meath. Newgrange dates from the Neolithic period (about 3200 BCE). It is widely recognised that the Neolithic cluster of centres at

The Neolithic burial mound at Newgrange, County Meath

Newgrange is evidence both of the extraordinary skill of our ancestors and of the existence of a spiritual dimension to their lives. The monuments are astronomically aligned and are related to the movement of the sun – an astonishing feat of engineering even by today's standards. The mound was used for burial as well as other rituals connected to the solstice. The stones are rich in carved symbols, known as megalithic art. Irish megalithic art is characterised by spirals and wavy lines among other shapes. These can be seen at Newgrange, particularly on the huge entrance stone. Scholars differ as to the precise meaning of these spirals. The fact that they occur in other similar sites in many different countries suggests that these shapes may have been universal symbols for the people of that era. Some scholars have suggested that spirals symbolise the cycle of life and are a celebration of the natural world. Others theorise that they symbolise the sun, moon and stars. There is compelling evidence to suggest that the Neolithic builders of Newgrange sought to be in harmony with the movement of the universe. Perhaps this offered them a sense of hope and optimism at a dark time of the year. Newgrange is

An example of megalithic art on a kerbstone at Newgrange

Resources for further study
See teacher's text on CD-Rom for further suggestions.

constructed so that on 21 December the rays of the rising sun pass through the shaft above the entrance and illuminate the inner chamber, filling it with splendid light. This occurs at the time of the year when the sun is at its lowest point. From that date on the days begin to lengthen. From the perspective of the people of that age, the sun had returned and darkness had been defeated.

The Neolithic people who built and used Newgrange struggled to express their deepest longings and fears about life and its mysteries. They sought to express their sense of something 'other', even something sacred, at the heart of life. Scholars have identified five categories of Palaeolithic symbols: all symbols; symbols of space; symbols of time; number symbols and symbols of story. What do these symbols tell us about religious behaviour in ancient societies?

Venus statuette

Figurines of animals and humans have been found in many archaeological sites. Of the human figures the 'Venus' statuettes, found in sites across Europe, are the most widely recognisable. Scholars differ as to their significance, but it is generally accepted that they possess a religious meaning. One interpretation is that at the time of death the figure of the fertile woman represented the hope of rebirth and resurrection. One scholar suggests that, '...Along with their wall paintings, cave sanctuaries, and burial sites, the female figurines of the peoples of the Palaeolithic are important psychic records. They attest to our forebears' awe at both the mystery of life and the mystery of death. They indicate that very early in human history the human will to live found expression and reassurance through a variety of rituals and myths...'[19]

The association of the feminine with the source of life is evident in many artefacts found at burial sites. 'For example, in the rock shelter known as Cro-Magnon in Les Eyzies, France (where in 1868 the first skeletal remains of our Upper Palaeolithic ancestors were found), around and on the corpses were carefully arranged cowrie shells. These shells ... seem to have been associated with some kind of early worship of a female deity.'[20]

57

1. What do you understand by sacred art and artefacts?
2. How old is Newgrange? What is this period in history called?
3. What do scholars believe to be the story of Newgrange?
4. 'Newgrange is rich in (sacred) art and artefacts.' Explain, using examples where possible.
5. What evidence of religious behaviour in ancient society do we get from such art and artefacts?

Assignments

1. Write a note on evidence of religious behaviour in ancient societies. Refer to symbols, burial rites, rites of passage, rites of initiation and sacrifice, sacred art and artefacts.
2. Research the archaeological site of Newgrange and find out about its structure, date and purpose. Make a copy of some of the symbols found there. Perhaps you could organise a visit for your class. Alternatively, there may be an ancient burial site in your own locality which you could visit and research.
3. What rituals of transition have most prominence in our society today? Write a note on why you think they are important.

Many of the symbolic objects and locations used by ancient societies in their burial rituals will remain mysterious to us. This is particularly the case in relation to societies that existed before the written word.

However, in many cases scholars have offered rich insights. For example, the placing of seeds in a tomb may suggest a belief in rebirth or resurrection. Red ochre is often found in Neolithic burials and it is thought by some to have religious significance; it may suggest the life-giving power of blood. Rich ornaments may indicate a belief in an afterlife or they may be an indication of the status of the person when alive. What we do know is that these rituals and symbols are evidence that ancient humans searched for meaning in the face of death and loss.

Rites of passage and initiation

Thanks to the development of sciences such as anthropology and archaeology in the nineteenth and twentieth centuries, we have begun to understand the development and use of ritual in ancient societies. At the beginning of the twentieth century the phenomenon of rites of passage was identified for the first time.

In the life of any individual there are times of transition and change. There are times when we must leave an old way of being and move on to the next stage, for example, birth, puberty, leaving home, marriage, and finally for us all, death. There are, of course, many more potential transitions one could face in the course of a lifetime, but those mentioned are significant for a majority of people. This was also the case for early humans. In considering marriage in relation to early humans we understand it in the broader sense of choosing a mate or partner. Research has shown that in ancient societies, such times of transition and change were marked by a special ritual. These rituals are called **rites of passage or initiation**. The existence of such rituals reveals the need people had to mark this change in status in a significant way. There is evidence to suggest that in some societies these rites were enacted in order to facilitate a change and a transition in the individual and/or the community and to place this transition in the larger context of the life cycle of birth-death-rebirth.

Rites of passage can be understood as another example of the early human need to understand and be in harmony with the cosmos, and as such can be considered early religious behaviour. There is a fundamental pattern underlying the rites of passage that have been discovered among different civilisations at different times in history, even though these rites may differ in terms of location and level of participation.[21] This pattern is characterised by three distinct elements:

Separation:
The individual is separated from peers/family/tribe, or the tribe separates from the place of day-to-day living.
Transition:
A ritual of transition is enacted. This may involve specially designated people from the group – parent, wise person, etc.
Incorporation:
Having changed, the individual rejoins the larger group, bringing a new way of seeing or living with them.

If you recall our earlier look at myth you will note that the three elements of rites of passage are also significant elements of some of the core myths. We will look now at the elements of a rite of passage in an ancient society. This is not a specific rite but a general picture incorporating the pattern outlined above.

A young girl may undergo a rite of passage to celebrate and mark in a ritualistic way her move from childhood to adulthood. This rite might take place at the onset of menstruation, when the girl is physically capable of reproduction. In ancient societies this time in the life of a girl had tremendous significance for the survival of the group and as such was surrounded with ritual and symbol. The girl would be separated from her family and group and would spend some period of time apart. There would be a special location for precisely this purpose – a cave, a shelter or a hut. The girl would be accompanied by a chosen adult, perhaps a wise woman or maybe her mother or older sister. There she would undergo a ritual or transition which might involve painting the body, wearing ceremonial robes, cutting her hair, etc. Special food might be eaten at this time. There might be praying and singing. The young girl might also get some instruction and advice about her role as an adult female. After a defined period of time, a day, a month or a week, the woman would return and be incorporated into her family and social group. She would no longer be a young girl – the girl she was has died and the woman she has become is born. Through this rite, a young girl made the transition to a new way of being in the world.

Woman and child and (below) a stag hunt. Cave paintings from Eastern Spain

Young boys would undergo a similar rite when it was time for them to enter the world of the adult male. In the case of the male rite of passage, the ritual would reflect the particular understanding of the role of men in that society. Perhaps the boy would have to undergo some dangerous task and prove his strength and bravery; this was most certainly the case in societies that depended on hunting for survival. It is interesting to note that the concept of adolescence did not exist in ancient societies; adolescence is a relatively recent invention. The whole idea of this

1. What are the significant moments that are celebrated/ recognised in society?
2. Were there religious elements present in ancient rites of transition? Explain.
3. Can you identify any examples of rituals of transition/initiation in our culture today? Do they follow the pattern outlined in this chapter?

Assignment

Design a rite of passage for one of the following using the information given in this chapter:

- A girl/boy about to finish secondary school.
- A man/woman preparing to marry.
- A boy/girl reaching the age of twenty-one.

Resources for further study
See teacher's text on CD-Rom for further suggestions.

This topic is also considered in **Section D, Moral Decision-Making** and **Section G, Worship, Prayer and Ritual**.

stage in development only came into existence in the latter half of the twentieth century. Today we recognise that young people need a number of years to make the transition from childhood to adulthood. Our ancestors marked this transition with a ritual. Modern societies continue to have their own rituals marking transitions, though in some cases they are not explicitly recognised as such.

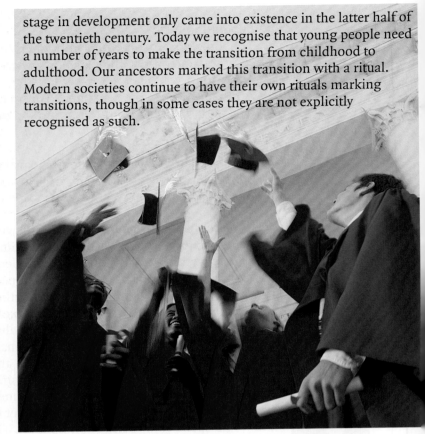

The Sense of the Sacred in Contemporary Culture

In his poem 'Advent', Patrick Kavanagh wrote:

'Through a chink too wide there comes in no wonder.'

He was commenting on the loss of a sense of mystery. Kavanagh longed to recapture the sense of awe and wonder that he had as a child. In our world today, with its scientific discoveries and technological advances, we could well ask if there is any wonder or mystery left. Compared to our ancient ancestors, we have incredible knowledge and understanding of our world and our cosmos. Things that were deeply mysterious to them are common knowledge to us. We know the earth is round – we have actually seen it! We understand the seasons and we know how we reproduce. However, advances in science and technology need not result in the loss of the sense of the sacred in our world. While we are very different to our ancient ancestors, in one respect we are the same – we still need to find meaning. Today people strive for happiness and fulfilment, most often through connection with others. How do human beings in the modern world continue to search for meaning? We are most aware of this

Can you think of examples from your own life or the lives of others in our society of 'transforming experiences'? Write about some of these examples.

spiritual quest when we experience something that challenges us to transform ourselves in some way. It might be the death of a loved one, reaching a certain age, the birth of a child, a serious illness, a national or international disaster, war, falling in love, overcoming an obstacle, tremendous beauty. These experiences force us to stop and reflect in order that we may understand them. This is as true for people in the modern world as it was for ancient societies. Despite the materialism, anger and violence that sometimes dominate our world, people continue to ask the questions and seek to understand. In fact, it could be argued that the noisier, more materialistic the world becomes, the deeper is the need for a sense of mystery, or the sacred.

The fundamental rituals of contemporary society have much in common with those of our predecessors. Funerals, weddings and christenings are significant across a wide variety of cultures. We grieve losses and celebrate joyful events. In doing so, we are naming the *sacred* in our lives. We mark significant transitions and acknowledge special achievements. We recognise the triumph over adversity. Poets and writers explore the deeper questions being asked by society.

Aran Island funeral

Prayer and pilgrimage are contemporary expressions of **spirituality** that point to an awareness of the sacred among people today. Prayer is a deeply instinctual spiritual practice. Many who may have rejected more traditional forms of prayer continue to seek ways of communicating with that which is beyond them. (Check out the Spirituality/Alternative section in any bookshop and there will be ample evidence of the interest in prayer and meditation. In contemporary culture there is an openness to Eastern practices like meditation and yoga. In our busy, crowded and noisy world it is not difficult to understand the need for silence. The practice of meditating in silence and stillness is a deeply spiritual experience for many people.)

Pilgrims on Croagh Patrick

Pilgrimage is an ancient spiritual practice. Today individuals and groups continue to travel to places that are significant or make journeys that in themselves are spiritual. In Ireland, many people travel to **Lough Derg** or climb Croagh Patrick. Both of these pilgrimages involve hardship and endurance, and for some it is these very qualities that make the pilgrimage a spiritual journey; they are forced to take stock and reflect on their lives, perhaps to seek forgiveness or to fulfil a promise.

Read the following introduction to a book about Lough Derg.

To 'do' Lough Derg is to form links with centuries of pilgrims who have come to Lough Derg exploring the issues that surface for every pilgrim in every age. ...

For thousands of years pilgrims have 'done' Lough Derg. Its survival to the present day can be described as a mystery, a miracle, a need, a challenge – all of these things – but most of all it is a place of pilgrimage. ...

Traditionally associated with bare feet and fasting, the entire pilgrimage is much greater than just popular headlines. The penitential practices undertaken make sense in hindsight – they are the pilgrimage, the challenge, the reparation, the lead up to the final morning – the third day – a true resurrection experience. Fasting begins from the midnight before commencing the pilgrimage, and continues until midnight on day three. There is a 'Lough Derg Meal' permitted once on each of the three days, when black tea or coffee, dry bread, toast or oatcakes are available.

On arrival to the Island, everyone removes their shoes and socks – bare feet are the dress code, and everyone immediately bonds in enduring the hardship of sharp stones and hidden surprises in muddy rock pools. ...

Nine stations are completed over three days. Each station, involving the constant repetition of familiar prayers around the remains of monastic cells – the penitential beds, located near the Basilica at the water's edge – moves the pilgrim into 'pilgrimage mode'.

The Vigil time is both the highlight and the challenge of the three days. Lack of sleep almost numbs the brain. The litany of repetitive prayers eventually becomes a **mantra** that forms part of the slowing down process and demands a concentration that removes day-to-day distractions. The sense of being in a place apart is compounded by the isolation and the bleakness of the location. Although just a short distance from the mainland, the boat journey across adds to the sense of journeying to a place apart. This is time alone, time to examine the realities of daily living, to seek a deeper relationship with self, community and God, in a space and a place tried and tested by pilgrims since the sixth century.[22]

Pilgrims at Lough Derg

Pilgrimages to Rome and the Holy Land are common and have particular significance for Roman Catholics. Pilgrimages to holy sites and shrines can be found throughout Ireland. Individuals may make their own personal pilgrimage to a special place in order to remember and commemorate, for example, to a grave, or a place of beauty that has particular significance. For many people today, nature is a source of spiritual nourishment; scenes of great beauty can fill us with a sense of wonder and awe. When people need to 'get away from it all'

Questions

1. What is a pilgrimage?
2. What does it mean to 'do' Lough Derg?
3. Why do you think so many people continue to make a pilgrimage to Lough Derg?
4. Can you think of any other pilgrimages that young people make today to get in touch with their inner selves?

they most often choose to go to somewhere of great natural beauty. This contemporary 'retreat' to nature is evidence of a sense of the sacred in the natural world. In this way we have something in common with traditional societies of the past; they too recognised the 'Creator' in the beauty of creation.

In contemporary culture, spirituality is seen in acts of kindness and charity between people. This ranges from the person who checks on an elderly neighbour to the many organisations run by volunteers who work on a daily basis to improve the lives of others. Across Ireland we can find people who work tirelessly for the good of others. Many do this because it gives meaning to their lives. The desire to connect with others in charitable work, in prayer, in discussions, in sacramental life and family life can be understood as a sign of a rich spirituality in today's world.

The following is an account of one young person's experience of being in Taizé in France.

Taizé is a very special place. Having no idea what Taizé was about, I went with open mind. The first thing that caught my eye when I arrived were the hundreds of young people there. But it seemed more than a gathering of young people for something like Féile or a holiday camp – there was an enormous sense of peace and joy that I had never experienced before.

Separated from the members of the group I had journeyed with, I was allocated my sleeping quarters, 'the barracks', to find that my quarters included twelve other people from Poland, Hungary, Germany, Lithuania and England. It was my first encounter with people from countries like Poland and Lithuania – that in itself was an experience. There was a language barrier, but for some reason verbal language was no great loss as a smile was often sufficient.

Our day there was time-tabled around three periods of prayer: morning, afternoon and evening. Here, hundreds of us gathered under one roof with the Taizé brothers, for an hour of prayer which included times of silence and of singing the Taizé chants. This was an experience to devour; here were hundreds of people from all over the world gathered together for essentially the same reason – our faith in God. It was quite a feeling, to say the least.

Assignments

. Give two examples of evidence of the sense of the sacred in contemporary culture.

.. Research one place of pilgrimage that is popular with (young) people today.

. Describe a place of great beauty that you have visited and say what is special about this place.

. Give an example of what you consider to be evidence of spirituality in action in today's world.

. Write about any Eastern religious practice that has become popular in our society.

Discuss

Why do you think acha calls Taizé a pecial place?

esources for further tudy

ee teacher's text on CD-Rom for further uggestions.

Between these periods of prayer, there were occasions when little groups would meet for a time of discussion and reflection. It was these moments that opened my eyes and heart the most. Across the language barrier a great sense of friendship and loyalty was immediately built. We talked about our relationship with God and religion in general. Each of us had our own personal doubts. God was/is present for us all no matter what part of the world we come from. We all realised and experienced this in some form and were willing to express it with those around us. Others questioned the validity behind 'believing' in the first place; they spoke of the lack of faith caused by a traumatic experience. Some had never thought much about it before. For the first time in my life, I realised that God was very much around me, all the time.

One thing I learnt during my stay in Taizé, and something which was strongly impressed on us by the brothers, was that our experiences of friendship and consideration for each other, and our openness to God, should not be confined to the perimeters of the Taizé village, but should continue when we went back home. I realise that these experiences can now also happen in Ireland, with my own friends and with the people I meet, at Mass, and in my relationship here and now with God.

Taizé is a place well worth visiting. You learn a lot about yourself and others, you can develop or acknowledge your relationship with God as a Christian and you certainly can have a lot of fun too!

P.S. I must also mention that the very fact that so many young people admitted their consideration for God in their lives (in comparison with young people I know in Ireland and in general) really gave me hope. Talking about our religion and faith should not be so stigmatised!

Sacha Fegan, Castleknock, Dublin

In summary

- Myth was an attempt by our ancestors to make sense of the great questions of life.

- Various rituals were devised to mark rites of passage/transition in people's lives.

- Some of these rituals had religious connotations.

- Despite contemporary materialism, there is still a sense of the sacred in contemporary culture.

- Think of going to Lough Derg or some other place of pilgrimage - and what this might mean to you.

- Religious and non-religious responses to the contemporary search for meaning abound.

The Humanist Tradition

You will learn about...

- humanism and humanists
- when humanism flourished and the factors that influenced this philosophy
- the beliefs of Erasmus, Marx and Camus
- cosmologies of modern science

'I think I lost my religion about, I couldn't tell you when. I just stopped believing. ...I believe it's a brilliant theory. It's a brilliant idea and it keeps society together and I'm very much in favour of it. But I believe more in people themselves and in the goodness of people than in saying it's all down to God....When there's something wrong I'll look to myself and to my friends and my family and ask them for help and rely on myself. I don't need to think that there is something there looking after me when I know that I have people who care for me and that I can look after myself.'
(Seventeen-year-old female)[23]

We have been exploring the human search for meaning and values as it takes place within a religious context. The term 'religious' refers to a fundamental belief that there is a 'sacred' or 'other' dimension to human existence. This view of life involves the belief that there is mystery to human existence, that human beings are created and have a deep connection to their creator. For religious persons this fundamental belief has implications for how they decide on right and wrong, how they treat others and the earth on which the live. However, the religious view of life is not the only view in contemporary culture. Throughout human history there have been many world views or systems of thought. In the context of the human desire to understand and find meaning, many paths to wisdom have been created and explained. These non-religious responses to the questions of life are sometimes in conflict with the religious responses and at other times they speak to each other. One such world view or philosophy is **humanism**.

The contemporary 'human-ist' position is that there is nothing higher than or other than human existence. This philosophy holds that within the human person is everything needed for a good and dignified life. Humanists believe that this life is all that we have and it is important to work at being happy and fulfilled. The happiness of others is also a concern for humanists. The fundamental position of humanism is that people are rational beings. Humanism is a way of thinking about humanity and the world that does not speculate on the existence of a creator or any divine being. Humanists deal with the great questions of life from a different perspective to religious persons. For humanists, these questions can be looked at with the use of reason and science. Consequently, humanism is a philosophy that does not deal with life after death. It is concerned with human needs and problems, with no reference to a higher power. **'Free thinking'** is a phrase associated with humanists. Humanism as a way of thinking can be traced as far back as the centuries preceding the Christian era. Thinkers and writers who adopted a humanist standpoint can be found at key moments in the history of civilisations. Ancient Greece, Rome, medieval Europe, all had humanist thinkers. It was in the period of time between the fourteenth and sixteenth centuries that humanism flourished. This was a time of rebirth and exploration in learning, which was characterised by the emergence of great thinkers; it is known as the **Renaissance** period. In this period there were many challenges to traditional ways of learning and thinking and a renewed confidence in the intellectual abilities of the person and their capacity to decide on what was right and wrong. The prevailing religious view did not go unchallenged. Initially, some of the most influential humanists were men of deep faith. However, as humanism developed, the belief in God or a higher power diminished.

Desiderius Erasmus (1466-1536)

Ironically, one of the great humanists of the Renaissance period was a cleric called Desiderius Erasmus. Erasmus was a devout Christian who was nevertheless critical of the Church of the day. He was born in Rotterdam in 1466 and was orphaned at a young age. He joined an Augustinian monastery and was ordained to the priesthood in 1492. Erasmus was a scholar and he travelled extensively around Europe. This was a turbulent and exciting time within the Church and within European society as a whole.

Between 1503 and 1511 Erasmus published documents calling for a spiritual renewal in the Church and within society. As a philosopher Erasmus believed in the power of education and he had much to say on the topic. He believed in the dignity of the human person and that education could be the means through which humans could improve and excel.

Scepticism (remember Nietzsche, on page 37) describes an attitude of questioning and withholding of judgement on an issue. It involves looking at all sides of an argument and then, if possible, making a judgement or decision. A sceptic believes that it is not possible to know the truth. Erasmus advocated skepticism with regard to issues of the day but he did not question the position of scripture as divine inspiration and, therefore, revealing truths. He was a Christian who drew much criticism because of his humanist views, even though he stopped short of challenging the Church directly. At this period in history the Church was entering one of its most turbulent times. Martin Luther was questioning certain teachings of the Church and a process had begun that would lead to the Reformation.

Karl Marx (1818-83) [24]

Karl Marx was born in Treves, Germany in 1818. After attending university he worked as a journalist in Europe and participated in the revolution in France in 1848. Marx was not a philosopher so much as a political theorist. However, he did study philosophy and his writing reveal his core belief about the nature of life, the role of the person and how meaning is found. While in London he made the acquaintance of Friedrich Engels, a factory manager who introduced him to the conditions of English workers. It was during his time in London that he wrote his most famous work, *Das Kapital*. The philosophy of Marx begins with the relationship between the person and the world. According to Marx, this world or environment is created by the work of humanity, individually and in social groups; it is human labour that creates history. Marx believed that the only unchanging element of human nature was the inclination to work and produce. His beliefs resulted in the theory of 'historical materialism', whereby the position a person held in the world of work and production determined their quality of life. This theory holds that humanity can be understood entirely through economics; that is, the value placed upon human labour and the product that results. From this standpoint Marx explained the development of human history.

In his later writings Marx identified work as the key area in which human beings found themselves alienated. This concept of alienation described the experience of having no sense of ownership or equal participation in work, resulting in feelings of not belonging and powerlessness. Masses of people worked for a relatively small wage (if any) and a few people controlled the means of producing goods; these same few held the majority of the profit. According to Marx, this was the primary source of inequality and suffering among people.

Marx had a vision of a society that was equitable and fair to all according to their abilities and needs. His vision of collective ownership and shared responsibility was a tribute to his faith in human potential. His philosophy reveals a deep respect for the dignity of the person and a belief in the possibility of an egalitarian, peaceful society.

Marx rejected religion and believed that human reasoning and consciousness were of the highest importance. He believed that the struggle for freedom was what made one human. Each person, according to Marx, had a desire and a need to reach their full potential and not be a slave to any system, whether this system was work or religion.

Marx devoted his life to writing about the human struggle for freedom. Through his writing he made a significant contribution to our understanding of society. [25]

What do you
understand by the
philosophy of
humanism?
When and why did
humanism develop?
Define scepticism as
used by Erasmus. Is
skepticism a feature
of life today?
In what sense
could Karl Marx
be considered a
humanist?
How did the
philosophy of
Camus develop?
Is Christian
humanism possible?

Albert Camus (1913–60)

Albert Camus was a French Algerian who was born into a poor working-class family. His philosophy grew out of this experience of being on the edge and separate. Because of his background he was very sensitive to discrimination on the basis of class and religion. He lived at a time of enormous change and turbulence in the world, particularly in Europe. The First World War had just begun at his birth and the Second World War was not long over by the time of

his death. In this context Camus developed a philosophy that was committed to the transformation of daily life. He believed that when the dignity of each individual was recognised and there was respect for human intelligence, then a meaningful society could be achieved. He equated what he saw as 'despair' in the world with the decline of traditional religion. He believed that there was an inbuilt desire to fight against this despair and bring about a transformation. His vision of the potential of the human being to bring about this transformation marks him as a significant figure in the humanist tradition. For Camus, rebellion against oppression was evidence of the human desire for dignity.

Three years before his death Camus was awarded the Nobel Prize for his work on understanding the human being and the universal human struggle to live a meaningful life.

In summary

- Humanism flourished between the fourteenth and sixteenth centuries, during the period known as the Renaissance.

- Erasmus believed in the importance of education and he encouraged questioning at all levels. This way of thinking is known as scepticism.

- Karl Mark believed in the importance of freedom for all. This freedom was to be obtained through the use of reason rather than through religious faith. He advocated that all the resources of society should be shared equally among all the members of society.

- The philosophy of Camus developed out of a wish to see the daily life of human beings transformed. Only when all are treated with dignity and respect will a meaningful society be achieved. He had a strong conviction about the potential of all human beings to change society for the better.

- Contemporary humanists believe that there is nothing greater than human existence.

- Humanists believe that people should work to create a world that cares for all the needs of humanity.

Non-religious Responses to the Questions of Life

You will learn about...
- the beliefs of secular humanism
  - atheism
  - agnosticism
  - reductionism

SECULAR HUMANISM

The origins of **secular humanism** or secularism can be traced to the Renaissance. However, it was in the seventeenth and eighteenth centuries, during the Enlightenment, that secular humanism took definite shape. For the humanists of the Enlightenment the purpose of human existence was the creation of a life and society that honoured the dignity of all. This, they believed, could be achieved through reason. Secular humanism did not believe in the goal of a blissful afterlife, but focused on creating fulfilment in this life. As a philosophy, secular humanism sometimes called secularism, has enormous confidence in the ability of human reason to understand and order the world. Scepticism is an important element of secular humanism. Socrates, the Greek philosopher, is the great example of a sceptic Socrates did not claim to know the 'truth' about anything; in fact, his claim was that he knew nothing. Earlier in this book you will have learned that Socrates used a method of questioning and dialogue as a means of learning. As a world view, secularism believes in science and reason as the ultimate source of knowledge and meaning. More accurately, secularism does not believe in anything that cannot be explained by science. In other words, secularism does not allow for a spiritual dimension to human fulfilment. The world view expressed by secularism is that human progress can be measured by how free it is from religious belief patterns. Secularism views religious belief as superstition. Science and the application of reason remove the necessity for such beliefs. On the other hand, the philosophy of secular humanism must also be noted for its vision of an open, tolerant society and its compassion for humanity.

ATHEISM[26]

Atheism is the denial of the existence of God. The absence of belief in the existence of God may be through deliberate choice or it may be a result of the inability to believe religious teachings. There are different types of atheism, depending on the reasons for non-belief.

Theoretical atheism is the denial of God's existence based on incompatible ideas or theories. For example, a theoretical atheist may find that science and religion are utterly incompatible. Another possible reason might be that the problem of evil and suffering in the world makes it impossible to believe in a loving God.

Practical atheism is a denial of God's existence because the question itself is of no relevance to the person. This form of atheism is also called **religious indifference.**

Militant atheism is the denial of God's existence based on the notion that religious belief is harmful and restricts human potential.

AGNOSTICISM

Agnosticism is the belief that we can only know what can be seen and understood using reason and science. In other words, agnosticism is the position of 'not knowing' when something cannot be explained by reason or science. The term was first used by the biologist T.H. Huxley (1825–95) in 1876. Huxley was a contemporary of Charles Darwin, whose theory of evolution challenged the prevailing Christian beliefs about creation. At the time Darwin's theory was radical and revolutionary. Huxley supported Darwin's theory and used the word 'agnostic' to describe his own position. Huxley believed that the question of whether a higher power existed remains unsolved and insoluble. Darwin's theory has been further developed by modern science and is now an accepted theory of evolution. The term agnostic continues to be used to describe the belief that the human mind cannot know anything that is beyond it. In contemporary society the term is used to describe those people who believe that evidence for or against God is inconclusive. Some agnostics believe that we can never know (strict agnoticism), while others take the position that we do not yet know (empirical agnosticism). Agnosticism is a form of skepticism. Scepticism in general questions whether the human person is capable of knowing the truth and, indeed, whether there is such a thing as 'the truth'.

REDUCTIONISM

Reductionism refers to the process of reducing an entity down to its smallest constituent parts. It began as a scientific method whereby scientists broke things down in order to learn more. For example, in chemistry and physics we began with earth, air, fire and water, but today we have sub-atomic theory, which reveals the minute parts of these elements and how they behave. Astronomy has progressed from the belief in a flat earth to the theory of an ever-expanding universe filled with galaxies. Science as we know it would not exist without this rational analysis. Reductionism as a world view emerged out of this kind of scientific enquiry. It can be applied to politics, art and language. However, when you apply this method to the question of what it means to be human and to the philosophical questions of life, then problems arise.

Reductionism refers to the belief that humans are part of the physical, natural world and no more than that. This world view holds that if something cannot be studied in a methodical, scientific way, then it cannot be known. Reductionism rules out speculation, opinion, feeling, superstition and belief as ways of coming to know truths. Essentially, reductionism reduces everything to its parts. A sentence is a collection of letters, spaces and punctuation marks. A novel is a collection of letters and no more. By reducing everything to its component parts, any higher level of meaning is lost. A novel is a story that can explore great themes and questions. A human being is more than a collection of atoms and DNA. Reductionism denies that we are more than the sum of our parts. Because this 'more' cannot be measured or analysed by scientific means, then it does not exist.

The idea that everything can be reduced to its simplest parts has consequences. In today's world there is a great demand for the short and simple approach to everything. Many of us have come to expect the 'sound bite' news and read the headlines rather than the article. We live in a culture that adores convenience in everything. *'Keep it simple and say it often'* could be seen as a reductionist philosophy. But sometimes things are not so simple and we are in danger of losing touch with more complex realities like what it means to be human, the meaning of justice and happiness, to name but a few.

In summary

- Secular humanists believe that human fulfilment is to be found in this life. They believe that science and reason are the ultimate sources of knowledge and meaning. In secular humanism there is no reference to an afterlife.

- Atheism is the denial of the existence of God.

- Agnosticism is the belief that if something, for example the existence of God, cannot be explained through reason or science, then it cannot be known.

- Reductionism is the belief that human beings are part of the physical world and no more than that. In reductionism there is no knowledge outside of methodical, scientific knowledge.

Resources for further study
See teacher's text on CD-Rom for further suggestions.

Cosmologies of Modern Science

You will learn about…
- the definition of cosmology
- modern theories regarding the origin of the universe
- the 'Big-Bang Theory' and 'The Expanding Universe Theory'

In the latter half of the twentieth century there were important discoveries in the field of physical science. Theories about space, time and matter changed in a fundamental way as a result of these discoveries. These new theories allowed scientists, philosophers and theologians to think anew about the origin of the universe and life itself. Historically, religion and science had a strained relationship. For almost all of human history people looked to religion to answer the great questions of life: how was the universe created? how will it end? how was life created? does it have a purpose? However, we have only to look to the fifteenth century to see that science sought to answer these very questions. Nicolaus Copernicus (1473–1543), (whom we already mentioned on page 34), laid the foundations for modern physics and astronomy. He believed that the earth revolves around the sun and also rotates on its own axis. This was in direct conflict with the religious understanding of the day. The religious view was that humans and the earth were at the centre of God's creation. Accordingly, everything was arranged around the earth. It took many years and much suffering on the part of supporters of Copernicus before his theory was accepted.

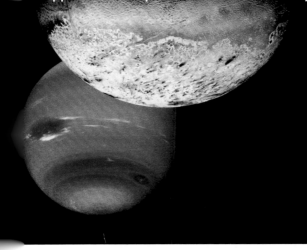

From these beginnings emerged an uneasy relationship between science and religion. Science and religion explore the deep questions of existence from completely different starting points. However, the theories of modern science do not replace a religious view. In some cases the two systems of thought can operate together in search of understanding. It is in the area of cosmology, the origin and nature of the universe, that science has much to reveal. The first question science asks is: was there a creation event or has the universe always existed? This is an important question and each answer begs further questions. If the universe always existed, then it is ageless or at least its age cannot be determined. Why do we find ourselves living in it now? If the universe had a definite moment of beginning, then we must accept that there was once nothing and then there was something. This suggests that there was a first moment, a creation event. If this is the case, what caused it?

The 'Big Bang' theory

Scientists, particularly cosmologists and astronomers, generally accept that there was a creation event. This occurred about eighteen billion years ago, when the world exploded into existence. This is commonly known as the 'Big Bang' theory. Scientists believe this to be the case because of one of the most fundamental laws of physics, the second law of thermodynamics. In its widest sense this law states that every day the universe becomes more and more disordered. There is a sort of gradual but inexorable descent into chaos. Examples of the second law are found everywhere: buildings fall down, people grow old, mountains and shorelines are eroded, natural resources are depleted.[27]

Is the world not full of examples that contradict this law? Babies are born, new buildings erected, order is restored. However, the second law applies to the system as a whole. According to this law the establishing of order in one part of the world has the effect of creating disorder somewhere else. The materials for a new building must have caused depletion or destruction elsewhere; the energy used is lost forever. Science argues and proves that according to this law, the world is moving toward disorder or chaos. What has this got to do with creation?

To return to *Sophie's World* once more, here is a snippet of conversation between Hilde and her father about the Big Bang and in particular the future of the universe:

> 'I'm trying to picture it.'
> 'If you have a balloon and you paint black spots on it, the spots will move away from each other as you blow up the balloon. That's what's happening with the galaxies in the universe. We say that the universe is expanding.'
> 'What makes it do that?'
> 'Most astronomers agree that the expanding universe can only have one explanation: Once upon a time, about 15 billion years ago, all substance in the universe was assembled in a relatively small area. The substance was so dense that gravity made it terrifically hot. Finally it got so hot and so tightly packed that it exploded. We call this explosion the Big Bang.'
> 'Just the thought of it makes me shudder.'[28]

Physicists came up with a means of measuring disorder within a system, known as **entropy.** Through experiments, they have shown that a system will eventually reach a level of entropy that means it can go no higher. This state is called thermodynamic equilibrium. If the universe is moving toward disorder, as this theory maintains, then it too must eventually reach the state of thermodynamic equilibrium. This leads to two undeniable conclusions. First, that the universe will die. Scientists call this the 'heat death' of the universe. Second, the universe cannot have existed forever because if it did it would have reached its end stage a long time ago. This law allows scientists to conclude that the universe did not always exist.

Scientists, particularly those involved in the physical sciences, have applied the second law of thermodynamics to the earth and the sun. In doing so they discovered that the temperature of the earth's core reveals that it is about four and a half billion years old. The sun is a little older and cannot burn forever; it is using up its fuel reserves. There is general agreement that the solar system came into existence at the same time. There is another compelling reason to believe that the universe had a distinct beginning; this concerns the force of gravity. Isaac Newton, one of the fathers of modern science, established that gravity was a universal force. Gravity acts on every element of the cosmos, between planets and stars. Why do they not fall together and crash into one another? Because planets revolve around the sun and the galaxy is rotating. This is called a centrifugal effect, which can be likened to the way the balls in a roulette wheel stay in place as long as it is turning; when the wheel stops turning the balls fall into the centre. There is no evidence that the universe as a whole is turning, so this present arrangement could not always have been so. How did it begin?

The 'Expanding Universe' theory

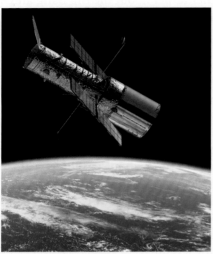

The Hubble Space Telescope in orbit above the Earth, courtesy European Space Agency

In the 1920s an American astronomer named Edwin Hubble discovered that the galaxies were not falling together but were moving apart. This theory is called the **'expanding universe' theory** of the cosmos. Simply put, if the universe is expanding, it must have been smaller at some time. The expansion rate is decelerating, which supports the view that there was an initial explosion that set the universe in motion. One more important dimension of modern cosmology is the theory that space itself was created in the 'Big Bang', and since space and time are inextricably linked, time itself was created at this moment. Time began at the Big Bang. The moment of creation was when space and time exploded out of nothing.

Scientists have discovered heat radiating from space, which is the residue of the intense heat created at the initial explosion or Big Bang. The Big Bang theory is now quite readily accepted by scientists and is welcomed by the majority of religious thinkers. Within the Big Bang theory there are different theories as to the nature of the universe and how it might end. There is no general agreement within the scientific community about the future of the universe. Science may have answered the question of whether or not a creation occurred, but what it has yet to discover is the cause of creation. Physicists continue to explore this question today.

In summary

- Cosmology is the study of the origin and nature of the universe.
  - The 'Big Bang' theory posits that the universe began about eighteen billion years ago with a big explosion.
  - The 'Expanding Universe' theory states that the universe is expanding all the time.

Questions

1. What is the relationship between Religion and Science with regard to the origin of the universe?
2. Who was Copernicus and what did he discover?
3. What is the first question asked by Science in relation to the creation of the universe?
4. What is the 'Big Bang' theory of creation?
5. What is the second law of thermodynamics?
6. What contribution did Isaac Newton make to the theory of creation?
7. What is the 'expanding universe' theory?

This topic is also considered in **Section J, Religion and Science**.

Oral/Written Revision of Important Terms

Look up the following terms which you have come across in **bold** type in this chapter and briefly explain each one: **myth, cosmos, sacred place, shaman, Tollund Man, sacred art and artefacts, rites of passage or initiation, spirituality, pilgrimage, Lough Derg, mantra, humanism, free thinking, Renaissance, secular humanism, atheism, religious indifference, agnosticism, reductionism, cosmology, 'big bang' theory, entropy, 'expanding universe' theory.**

Part Three: Concepts of God

We have received this gift from the hands of SOMEONE.

(Alexander Solzhenitsyn)

Chapter 5: The Gods of the Ancients

In this chapter you will learn about...

- ● the concept of God in ancient times
- ● the gods of the ancients as depicted in myth
- ● polytheism and the emergence of monotheism
- ● the concept of God in the great monotheistic religions

Read the following song lyrics and discuss the questions.

From A Distance *by Nanci Griffith*

From a distance the world looks blue and green
and the snow-capped mountains white.
From a distance the ocean meets the stream
and the eagle takes to flight.

From a distance there is harmony
and it echoes through the land.
It's the voice of hope. It's the voice of peace.
It's the voice of every man.

From a distance we all have enough
and no one is in need.
There are no guns, no bombs, no disease,
no hungry mouths to feed.

From a distance we are instruments
marching in a common band,
Playing songs of hope, songs of peace,
They're the songs of every man.

God is watching us. God is watching us.
God is watching us from a distance.

From a distance you look like my friend
even though we are at war.
From a distance I can't comprehend
what all this war is for.

From a distance there is harmony and it
echoes through the land.
It's the hope of hopes.
    It's the love of loves.
        It's the heart of every man.[29]

Redemption Song *by Bob Marley*

Old pirates yes they rob I
Sold I to the merchant ships
Minutes after they took I from the
Bottom less pit
But my hand was made strong
By the hand of the almighty
We forward in this generation triumphantly
All I ever had is songs of freedom
Won't you help to sing these songs of freedom
Cause all I ever had, redemption songs, redemption songs

Emancipate yourselves from mental slavery
None but ourselves can free our minds
Have no fear for atomic energy
Cause none of them can stop the time
How long shall they kill our prophets
While we stand aside and look
Some say it's just a part of it
We've got to fulfil the book

Won't you help to sing, these songs of freedom
Cause all I ever had, redemption songs, redemption songs,
redemption songs

Emancipate yourselves from mental slavery
None but ourselves can free our minds
Have no fear for atomic energy
Cause none of them can stop the time
How long shall they kill our prophets
While we stand aside and look
Yes some say it's just part of it
We've got to fulfil the book

Won't you help to sing these songs of freedom
Cause all I ever had, redemption songs
All I ever had, redemption songs
These songs of freedom, songs of freedom[30]

Questions

1. What is the image of God in each song?
2. What qualities are attributed to God?
3. Which images of God in these lyrics appeal to you? Why?
4. Describe the relationship between God and humanity expressed in each song.

The concept of a God is common to all religions. From the very beginning people had an idea of a God or gods who created the world, and they worshipped these gods in different ways. The concept of God developed and progressed as human beings developed and learned more about the world in which they lived. The idea of God changed from a mythical understanding to a more rational understanding. People's history influenced their understanding of God. We will see this in the experience of the Israelites. In patriarchal societies, where the male/father role dominated, images of God are often male images. In agricultural societies the images and understanding of God are linked to the land and the cycle of the seasons. Each generation in every culture faced the big questions of life. Their experience of life and their knowledge shaped the 'answers' and their understanding of God.

> Humanity's continuing search for meaning and values has influenced the concept of God within the various cultures.

The Gods of the Ancients

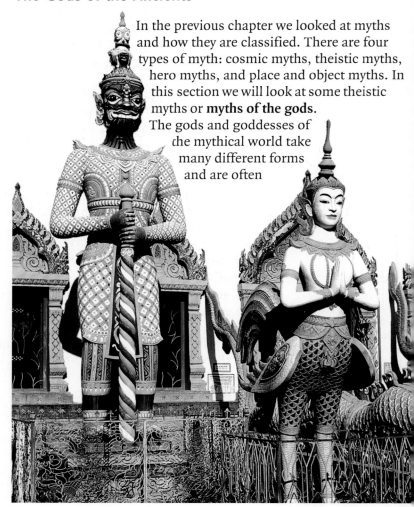

In the previous chapter we looked at myths and how they are classified. There are four types of myth: cosmic myths, theistic myths, hero myths, and place and object myths. In this section we will look at some theistic myths or **myths of the gods**. The gods and goddesses of the mythical world take many different forms and are often fascinating. They often share characteristics, even when they are from widely differing cultures. These characteristics identify a 'type' of god, and are called **archetypes**. For example:

> **Father/creator god**
>
> Great mother
>
> **Dying god**
>
> Trickster
>
> **Destroyer god**
>
> Helper god
>
> **Male/Female pair**
>
> Gods who visit the earth and are shunned

'**Pantheon**' is the word used to describe the officially recognised gods of a particular culture. The pantheon gives us an insight into the values and mindset of a people. For example, the Greek pantheon tells us much about the concerns of Greek civilisation and how the ancient Greeks understood themselves and the world. The Egyptian pantheon reveals what was important to the Egyptians at the time their myths were created, and so on. The mythology of cultures like Egypt, Greece and Rome has given us a wealth of familiar gods and goddesses, but it is important to remember that other cultures also have mythological characters.

While there are many gods and goddesses in the Greek pantheon, twelve principal gods emerge as the most important. These comprise of Zeus and his family, who lived on **Mount Olympus** and were thought to rule the world.

> **Zeus,** the leader of the family of gods
> **Hera,** his wife, the goddess of marriage
> **Ares,** the god of war
> **Hephaestus,** the god of fire and metal-working
> **Aphrodite,** goddess of love and beauty
> **Artemis,** goddess of wild beasts and hunting
> **Apollo,** god of music, poetry and art
> **Demeter,** goddess of agriculture and harvest
> **Hestia,** goddess of the hearth and family life
> **Poseidon,** god of the sea and earthquakes
> **Athene,** goddess of war and wisdom
> **Hermes,** messenger of the gods and god of travellers

Discuss

Do you know of any stories about the ancient gods and goddesses? Tell the story in your own words. What do these stories tell you about the gods and goddesses involved?

The gods of the ancient myths were feared rather than loved by the people of the time. They had great powers but they often displayed the weaknesses and faults seen in ordinary human beings. For example, the Greek God Zeus was strong and powerful; he was a father, husband and head of the family; however, Zeus also had the failings of a mortal man. Zeus was a sky god, concerned particularly with the weather, and his standard was a thunderbolt. The following myth concerning Zeus tells us something of his character.

Zeus – The Father of Heaven

Only Zeus, the Father of Heaven, might wield the thunderbolt; and it was with the threat of its fatal flash that he controlled his quarrelsome and rebellious family on Mount Olympus. He also ordered the heavenly bodies, made laws, enforced oaths, and pronounced oracles. When his mother Rhea, foreseeing what trouble his lust would cause, forbade him to marry, he angrily threatened to violate her. Though she at once turned into a menacing serpent, this did not daunt Zeus, who became a male serpent and, twining around her in an indissoluble knot, made good his threat. It was then that he began his long series of adventures in love. He fathered the Seasons and the Three Fates of Themis; the Charities on Eurynome; ...he lacked no power above or below earth; and his wife Hera was equal to him in one thing alone: that she could still bestow the gift of prophecy on any man or beast she pleased.

A time came when Zeus' pride and petulance became so intolerable that Hera, Poseidon, Apollo, and all the other Olympians, except Hestia, surrounded him suddenly as he lay asleep on his couch and bound him with rawhide thongs, knotted into a hundred knots, so that he could not move. He threatened them with instant death, but they had placed his thunderbolt out of reach and laughed insultingly at him. While they were celebrating their victory, and jealously discussing who was to be his successor, Thetis the Nereid, foreseeing a civil war on Olympus, hurried in search of the hundred-handed Briareus, who swiftly untied the thongs, using every hand at once, and released his master. Because it was Hera who had led the conspiracy against him, Zeus hung her up from the sky with a golden bracelet about either wrist and an anvil fastened to either ankle. The other deities were vexed beyond words, but dared attempt no rescue for all her piteous cries. In the end Zeus undertook to free her if they swore never more to rebel against him; and this each in turn grudgingly did. Zeus punished Poseidon and Apollo by sending them as bond-servants to King Laomedon, for whom they built the city of Troy; but he pardoned the others as having acted under duress.[31]

Questions

1. What faults did Zeus display?
2. What did the Olympians do to Zeus?
3. How was Zeus rescued?
4. What kind of god was Zeus?
5. What human weaknesses did this myth seek to explain?

The gods that emerged from Northern and Western Europe were gods of thunder, rain and wind. Perhaps this reflected the colder, darker atmosphere of this part of the world. This is an example of how the culture of a people affected their understanding of God. The mythology of the Nordic culture is one that depicts the

constant struggle against the forces of darkness and chaos. The Nordic gods often engaged in violent battles against the forces of evil, which were depicted as giants and monsters. They have left us with a treasure of exciting and bloody adventures! Odin was the father of the gods of Norse mythology. He was said to have only one eye, to be fierce in battle but wise in times of peace. He is often depicted riding across the sky on an eight-legged horse.

Thor is probably one of the best known of the Nordic gods. He was the god of thunder. He is described as a huge red-bearded figure, who was armed with a hammer, iron gloves and a girdle of strength. He was an outspoken god, with an enormous appetite for food and drink. The story that follows gives us some insights into this colourful Nordic god.

The Story of Thor

The myth that is best known in the Nordic countries comes from the Eddic poem 'The Lay of Thrym'. It tells how Thor, rising from sleep, finds that his hammer is gone. This makes him so angry that his hands tremble and his beard shakes. Accompanied by his henchman Loki, he goes to Freyja to ask if Loki may borrow her wings so that he can fly to Jotunheim, the land of the giants, and find out if they are the ones who have stolen Thor's hammer.

At Jotunheim Loki meets Thrym, the king of the giants, who sure enough begins to boast that he has hidden the hammer seven leagues under the earth. And he adds that the gods will not get the hammer back until Thrym is given Freyja as his bride.

Loki returns to Asgard and tells Freyja to put on her wedding attire for she is (alas) to wed the king of the giants. Freyja is furious, and says people will think she is absolutely man-crazy if she agrees to marry a giant.

Then the god Heimdall has an idea. He suggests that Thor dress up as a bride. With his hair up and two stones under his tunic he will look like a woman. Understandably Thor is not wildly enthusiastic about the idea, but he finally accepts that this is the only way he will ever get his hammer back.

So Thor allows himself to be attired in bridal costume, with Loki as his bridesmaid.

When the gods arrive at Jotunheim, the giants begin to prepare the wedding feast. But during the feast the bride – Thor, that is – devours an entire ox and eight salmon. He also drinks three barrels of beer. This astonishes Thrym. The true identity of the god is very nearly revealed. But Loki manages to avert the danger by explaining that Freyja has been looking forward to coming to Jotunheim so much that she has not eaten for a week. When Thrym lifts the bridal veil to kiss the bride, he is startled to find himself looking into Thor's burning eyes. Once again Loki saves the situation by explaining that the bride has not slept for a week because she was so excited about the wedding. At this, Thrym commands that the hammer be brought forth and laid in the bride's lap for the wedding ceremony. Thor roars with laughter when he is given the hammer. First he kills Thrym with it, and then he wipes out the giants and all their kin. And thus the gruesome hostage affair has a happy ending.[32]

We can look at this myth as a story that the people used to explain something that they did not understand. Thor is the god of thunder and he has a huge appetite; perhaps this story of the loss of his hammer explained crop failure or drought. Thor recovers his hammer; this could be the coming of spring.

'But a myth was not only an explanation. People also carried out religious ceremonies related to the myths. We can imagine how people's response to drought or crop-failure would be to enact a drama about the events in the myth.'[33]

As we have seen in earlier chapters, myths served an important purpose in the ancient world: they explained what life was all about. However, as the world developed and progressed, human beings began to look elsewhere for the answers to life's questions. Around the sixth century BCE the Greeks began to think in a new way about the questions of life. Men like Socrates, Plato and Aristotle developed theories on the meaning of life. This new approach, called philosophy, represented a break from the mythic understanding of life and was to influence the thinking of the Western world for generations to come.

Questions

1. What kind of god was Thor?
2. How do you think this myth could have been re-enacted in ancient times?
3. What questions was this myth trying to answer for our ancestors?

Assignments

1. Outline briefly the story of Thor.
2. Compare this myth with the Greek myth of Zeus.

Polytheism

The belief in many gods is called **polytheism.** Polytheism is the norm rather than the exception in the religions of the world today. The three great exceptions to this rule are Judaism, Christianity and Islam. These are the three classical monotheistic religions. **Monotheism** means the belief in one God. Monotheism and polytheism refer to the understanding of the transcendent within a religion. The **transcendent** refers to the belief in a higher power, the other, the sacred – generally referred to as God. *(We will be looking at different understandings of the transcendent later in chapter 6.)*

Hinduism

Hinduism is an example of a polytheistic religion. Hindus believe in a number of gods. This religion originated in India around 2500 BCE. What we now understand as Hinduism began as a collection of different religious beliefs and practices, which developed over the past four thousand five hundred years. Hinduism strives to achieve freedom for its members. This liberation is known as *moksha*. **Moksha** is the release from the cycle of birth, death and rebirth. Each person is believed to have a soul, known as *atman*. This soul can be born millions of times into millions of forms or incarnations. Believers want to be freed from all worldly attachments, and they can only achieve this liberation by living good lives in each successive life. Their ultimate goal is to be delivered into eternity, known as **Brahman**, the god-head, the source and origin of all creation. Hindus believe that Brahman is the ultimate source of their existence. Brahman is a distant, all-powerful god who has to be approached through a number of more accessible deities, the principal ones being:

This topic is also considered in **Section C, World Religions**.

Brahma
the creator who brings the Universe into existence

Vishnu
who preserves life and all living things

Shiva
who destroys the world

Assignments

1. Write a brief description of Hinduism and explain how it is a polytheistic religion.
2. Research Hinduism under the following headings:
   History
   Practice
   Geographical location
   Central gods/goddesses
   Images associated with Hinduism

This Hindu trinity represents the cycle of creation, preservation and destruction, which is the centre of Hindu belief. The goddess **Mahadeiri** is also a principal deity in Hinduism. Hindus frequently have a favourite deity and they may have a shrine to them in their homes.

The **Puranas** is the sacred text within Hinduism; it tells the story of creation and the lives of the gods.

Hindus believe that there are four stages one must go through in order to achieve moksha. These are:

- **Being a student** – to learn about the sacred literature
- **Being a householder** – to develop responsibility in society
- **Being a contemplative** – to reflect and meditate on important things in life
- **Being an ascetic** – to renounce the pleasures of the world

Shinto

Another example of polytheism is found in the Japanese religion called **Shinto**. This religion originated in prehistoric Japan and has a long and complex history. Shinto does not have a founder or indeed a particular doctrine. It is practised by many Japanese as a folk religion, often alongside Buddhism. In the nineteenth and twentieth centuries there were efforts to rid Shinto of its Buddhist influences. As a result, 'State Shinto' emerged around 1868. Shinto lost its status as the religion of the Japanese State in 1945.

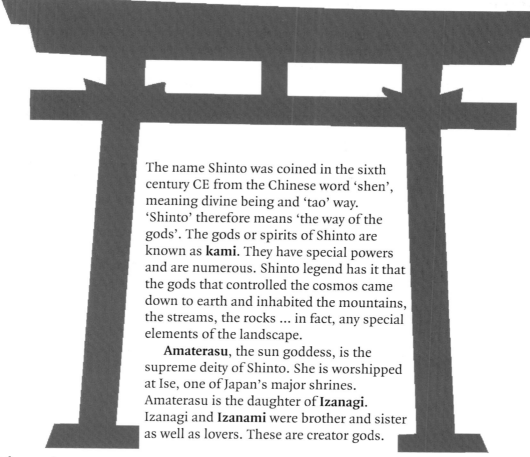

The name Shinto was coined in the sixth century CE from the Chinese word 'shen', meaning divine being and 'tao' way. 'Shinto' therefore means 'the way of the gods'. The gods or spirits of Shinto are known as **kami**. They have special powers and are numerous. Shinto legend has it that the gods that controlled the cosmos came down to earth and inhabited the mountains, the streams, the rocks ... in fact, any special elements of the landscape.

Amaterasu, the sun goddess, is the supreme deity of Shinto. She is worshipped at Ise, one of Japan's major shrines. Amaterasu is the daughter of **Izanagi**. Izanagi and **Izanami** were brother and sister as well as lovers. These are creator gods.

Assignments

1. Write a note on the Shinto religion, explaining its origin and core practices.
2. Explain how Shinto may be identified as a polytheistic religion. Refer to the beliefs and practices associated with Shinto.
3. Research the Shinto religion under the following headings:
   History
   Geographical location
   Current status as a world religion
   Core beliefs and practices
   Images associated with Shinto

Followers of Shinto worship their gods at shrines known as *jinja* and this worship is carried out using very precise rituals. Shinto has special religious experts known as **shamans**, whose job is to ensure that the rituals are carried out correctly, something that is very important to the believers of Shinto.

The other spirits (*kami*) of Shinto are also honoured and worshipped, and believers ask the kami for favours and blessings. The purpose of Shinto is to come to know the wishes of the kami and to carry out these wishes. A devout follower of Shinto sees every day as an opportunity to be of service (*matsumi*) to the kami. Shinto religion has a positive view of the human person. It is believed that humans and all of nature are children of the kami and, therefore, are fundamentally good. Many of the rituals of Shinto are intended to cleanse the person so that this inherent goodness comes through.

Monotheism

As time went by, certain people and groups began to move from polytheism to a belief in the existence of one supreme God. This understanding of the transcendent did not happen overnight; in fact, it involved a slow and often confused shift in the belief patterns of the people involved. The man principally associated with the move from polytheism to monotheism is **Abraham**. Abraham and his family lived

some time between 2000 and 1500 BCE and they inhabited the area known as The Fertile Crescent in the ancient Near East. This land stretched from Mesopotamia in the east to Egypt in the west. Canaan was the fertile landmass between Mesopotamia and Egypt. It was to this land that a great many nomadic people came in the hope of finding a place where they could settle and develop a more stable way of life. Abraham was one of these nomads.

Genesis 11:31 tells us that Abraham, his father Terah and his wife Sarah, along with his nephew Lot, left the city of Ur in Mesopotamia for the land of Canaan. They settled in Haran and remained there until Terah's death. On the death of Terah, Abraham became the leader of the family. We are told in Genesis, chapter 12, that, after the death of his father, Abraham was instructed by the Lord:

'Go from your country and your kindred and your father's house to the land that I will show you.'

The Lord promised Abraham:
'I will bless you, and make your name great, so that you will be a blessing.
I will bless those who bless you, and the one who curses you I will curse; and in you all the families of the earth shall be blessed.' (Genesis 12:1-3)

Abraham went as the Lord directed him, and Lot went with him. When Abraham, Sarah, Lot and the others arrived in Shechem in Canaan, the Lord spoke to Abraham:
'To your offspring I will give this land.' (Genesis 12:7)

So Abraham built an altar there to the Lord, who had appeared to him. Thus began the special relationship between **Yahweh** and the Israelites. The books of Genesis and Exodus tell us a great deal about the adventures of Abraham and his descendants in their struggle to come to terms with belief in one God in a culture permeated by a belief in many gods. Even in the final chapters of Exodus, written in the fifth century BCE, we are told of God's **covenant** with Moses on Mount Sinai. The very idea of a 'covenant' or agreement with God tells us that polytheism was still alive and well. A covenant with

Yahweh was only necessary because worship of other gods was threatening the people's total loyalty to the one true God. It appears that the Israelites thought that Yahweh was one god among others. It was through their covenant with Yahweh that they pledged their allegiance to Yahweh alone. Throughout the **Pentateuch** (the first five books of the Old Testament) there is evidence that the people of Israel assumed that there were other gods in existence. The Ten Commandments reveal this assumption:

This topic is also considered in **Section C, World Religions**.

> I am the Lord your God, who brought you out of the land of Egypt,
> out of the house of slavery; you shall have no other gods before me.
> (Deuteronomy 5:6-7)

The Axial Age

The history of the Israelites shows how reluctant they were to put all their trust in one God. Even while Moses was on Mount Sinai receiving the Ten Commandments, the 'chosen people' had already turned back to the pagan religion of Canaan. They fashioned a golden calf (the traditional symbol of the pagan god El) and adored it. So while religious leaders like Moses preached strict monotheism, the people often wandered back to the older rituals that worshipped a variety of gods. They feared that neglect of the other gods might be foolish. Yahweh was seen as being very powerful in times of war and it was in these times that devotion to Yahweh was strong, but in times of peace the Israelites often reverted to worship of pagan gods such as Baal, Anat and Asherah. The period between 800 and 200 BCE, known as the **Axial Age**, was the time when monotheism became firmly established. Belief in one God was to become crucial in the development of the three major monotheistic religions that exist today. The Axial Age was a time of great prosperity, which led to intellectual and cultural developments that have had an enormous impact on the course of history. The God of the Israelites that emerged in the Axial Age was a military God, who demanded both outward practice and an inward belief and allegiance to him. The sin of **idolatry** (the worship of false gods) became a deadly sin for Jewish people. They understood Yahweh as an all-powerful yet compassionate God, who demanded complete loyalty in return for his great love. As the circumstances of the Jewish people changed and they were faced with hardship, their belief in only one God was very important to them, as it reinforced their sense of themselves as different. Their status as the chosen people of Yahweh became a source of hope for them.

Stone slab depicting the god Baal

God in Judaism

The most distinctive aspect of the Jewish faith is the belief that God is connected to the Jewish people in a special and unique way. Jews understand themselves as God's chosen people. Yahweh's covenant with them is the foundation of their concept of God.

The God of Abraham, Isaac and Jacob was a military God. Yahweh promised Abraham and his descendants that he would make them into a great nation. The Jews believed that their God was a very powerful God and they could not look upon his face or speak his name. Yahweh was distant but he loved his people. The Jewish people knew that in times of war and danger they could depend on Yahweh for military success. At this point in Jewish history, Yahweh could be described as a tribal God of war, who favoured the Israelites and would help them to secure the Promised Land. The story of Moses and the Exodus reveal God as a liberator.

The understanding of Yahweh did, however, change and develop over time. The Yahweh of the Axial Age was no longer just a military God. After much pain and struggles, Yahweh became a symbol of total transcendent power. Yahweh was now understood as the one true God, not one god among others. For the Jewish people, God was a compassionate God who loved his people and who required more than the appearance of loyalty. Outward signs of obedience were not enough. According to Deuteronomy 6:4-6, Yahweh required total, sincere and exclusive devotion. They were to worship no other gods. This understanding of God had consequences for the Jewish people. They were now required to live in a certain way. God was seen as a compassionate and just God, and so now the people of God had to behave in a similar way. This call to compassion and justice can be seen in the writings of the prophets.

Assignment

Read Exodus 3:1-9. What image of God is revealed in this passage? What do we learn about the Jewish understanding of God from this passage?

It was during the time of the Babylonian exile, 587-539 BCE, that the concept of Yahweh as the one and only God became deeply ingrained in the Jewish religious psyche. The Jews now came to see God as extremely powerful. The creation stories from Genesis were written around this time and they describe an all-powerful God who created the universe and brought order to chaos. Perhaps it is no coincidence that such writings would emerge at a time of such despair for God's people.

God in Christianity

The Christian understanding of God has come from the Jewish God of the Old Testament. Christians believe in an all-powerful creator God, as do the Jews. The creation stories found in the book of Genesis are common to both traditions. Christians believe in a personal God who loves his people and requires their love in return. The God of Christianity is a forgiving and merciful God. The image of Father (**Abba**) is central to the Christian understanding of God. The word 'Abba' was the word used by Jesus to describe his relationship with God. It is an intimate term that describes a father-child relationship. It is often compared to the English word 'dad' or 'daddy'. It describes a loving, paternal relationship between God and God's people. Christians believe that God revealed himself in a unique way through his Son, Jesus Christ. They believe that God became flesh in and through the person of Jesus. Through his life, death and resurrection, Jesus revealed God to us in a special and unique way. This revelation is

The Rublev icon of the Trinity

Assignment

Read the following excerpts from the Nicene Creed and answer the questions.

We believe in one God,
the Father, the Almighty,
maker of heaven and earth,
of all that is, seen and unseen.

We believe in one Lord, Jesus Christ,
the only Son of God,
eternally begotten of the Father,
God from God,
Light from Light,
true God from true God,
begotten, not made,
of one Being with the Father…

We believe in the Holy Spirit,
the Lord, the giver of life,
who proceeds from the Father and the Son.
With the Father and the Son he is worshipped and glorified.
He has spoken through the Prophets.

1. What image of God is revealed in this Creed?
2. What does it reveal about the Christian understanding of God?

understood by Christians to be a saving event. After Jesus' **ascension** into heaven, he was no longer visible in the world. Christians believe that God then communicated with humanity through the **Holy Spirit**, who descended on Christ's disciples at Pentecost. The Christian concept of God is expressed as belief in the three persons of Father, Son and Holy Spirit, known as the **Trinity.** It is important to understand that Christians believe in one God in three persons, each of whom is equally divine and only one of whom (Jesus, the Son of God) became incarnate (literally 'enfleshed'). The Trinitarian understanding of God was formalised at the Council of Nicaea in 325 and is expressed in the **Nicene Creed**.

God in Islam

The God of Islam is known as **Allah** and he is believed to be the same God as the God worshipped by Jews and Christians. The oneness of God is central to Islam. The **Qur'an** is the sacred book of the Islamic faith and it contains the word of God as revealed to **Muhammad**, the great prophet, during the seventh century. The Qur'an is extremely important to Muslims, as it is the ultimate source of Allah's revelation to his people. They believe that it is through the Qur'an that they can come to know the will of Allah.

Muslims believe that God is so great and so 'other-worldly' that human beings will never fully know him. For Muslims, Allah is the creator of all things. He is all-powerful and is more impersonal than the God of Judaism and Christianity. Allah is an incomprehensible God and in many ways is inaccessible. However, Allah is revealed through the world and through the words of the Qur'an. Muslims believe that Allah is a merciful and generous God. They see nature as Allah's great gift to them. The word 'merciful' is used extensively in the Qur'an to describe Allah. Allah is also seen as the great and just Judge. Muslims believe that

Read the following
passage from the Qur'an
and answer the questions.

> He is God: there is no
> god but He.
> He is the Knower of the
> unseen and the visible;
> He is the all-Merciful,
> the all-Compassionate.
>
> He is God, there is no
> god but He.
> He is King, the all-Holy,
> the all-Peaceable,
> the all-Faithful,
> the all-Preserver,
> the all-Mighty,
> the all-Compeller,
> the all-Sublime.
> Glory be to God, above
> that they associate.
>
> He is God, the Creator,
> the Maker, the Shaper.
> To him belongs the
> Names Most Beautiful.
> All that is in the
> heavens and the earth
> magnifies Him.
> He is the all-Mighty, the
> all-Wise. (Q.59:22-24)

1. What image of God is
   revealed in this
   passage?
2. What does this
   passage tell us about
   the image of God
   in Islam?

Assignments

1. Explain what you
   understand by
   polytheism and
   monotheism.
2. Describe briefly the
   emergence of
   monotheism.
3. Explain the concept of
   God in each of the
   monotheistic traditions:
   Judaism, Christianity
   and Islam.
4. Compare and contrast
   the concept of God in
   two of these traditions.

on the Last Day Allah will judge them, and this judgement will depend on their belief in Allah and in his messenger, Muhammad.

Faith in Allah and commitment to the Islamic faith demands total submission and surrender to the will of God, and for the devout Muslim the Qur'an offers the blueprint for that submission and salvation.

In summary

- Theistic myths or myths of the gods tried to enshrine the concept or idea of god for ancient peoples.
- Polytheism is the belief in many gods, as exemplified by Hinduism and the Shinto religion.
- Monotheism – the belief in one God – gradually emerged during the lifetime of Abraham.
- The three great monotheistic religions are Judaism, Christianity and Islam.

Oral/Written Revision of Important Terms

Look up the following terms which you have come across in **bold** type in this chapter and briefly explain each one:
myths of the gods, archetypes, pantheon, Mount Olympus, polytheism, monotheism, transcendent, Hinduism, moksha, atman, Brahman, Mahadeiri, Puranas, Shinto, kami, Amaterasu, Izanagi and Izanami, shaman, Abraham, Yahweh, covenant, Pentateuch, Axial Age, idolatry, Abba, ascension, Holy Spirit, Trinity, Nicene Creed, Allah, Qu'ran, Muhammad.

Earth's crammed with heaven and every common bush afire with God: But only he who sees, takes off his shoes; The rest sit round it, and pluck blackberries.

(Elizabeth Barrett Browning)

Chapter 6: The Concept of Divine Revelation

In this chapter you will learn about...

● the meaning of divine revelation and how it is understood in the major world religions

● the impact of the concept of divine revelation on religious practice in Judaism, Christianity and Islam

● the impact of the concept of divine revelation on the interpretation of religious texts in Judaism, Christianity and Islam

● the meaning of the transcendent and the contrasting understanding of this in Christianity and Islam

The Face of God

John Jackson, a photographer with the *Indianapolis Star*, was sent to Ecuador in 1987 to cover the earthquake that devastated much of the country. In the midst of such catastrophic suffering he witnessed a simple scene of compassion.

> The line was long but moving briskly.
> And in that line, at the very end
> stood a young girl about twelve years of age.
> She waited patiently
> as those in the front of that long line
> received a little rice, some canned foods or a little fruit.
> Slowly but surely
> she was getting closer to the front of that line,
> closer to the food.

From time to time she would glance across the street.
She did not notice the growing concern
on the faces of those distributing the food.
The food was running out.
Their anxiety began to show but she did not notice.
Her attention seemed always to focus on three figures
under the trees across the street.
At long last she stepped forward to get her food.
But the only thing left was a lonely banana.
The workers were almost ashamed to tell her
that was all that was left.
She did not seem to mind to get that solitary banana.
Quietly she took the precious fruit and ran across the street
where three small children waited – perhaps her sisters and a brother.
Very deliberately she peeled the banana
and very carefully divided the banana into three equal parts.
Placing the precious food into the eager hands
of those three younger ones –
one for you, one for you, one for you –
she then sat down
and licked the inside of that banana peel.
In that moment, I swear,
I saw the face of God.[34]

In the last chapter we spent some time exploring the many concepts of God in myth, in some of the polytheistic religions, and, finally, in the three major monotheistic religions. Each belief system has its own unique image and understanding of the **transcendent.** (To transcend means to go beyond or extend normal

God is in the
bits and pieces
of Everyday –
A kiss here and
a laugh again,
and sometimes
tears,
A pearl necklace
round the neck
of poverty.

(Patrick Kavanagh)[35]

This topic is also
considered in **Section H,
The Bible: Literature
and Sacred Text**.

The Torah

boundaries. And in the religious sense, a transcendent God extends to the spiritual or unknowable dimension of reality. We will return to the understanding of the transcendent in some religious traditions later in this chapter.) Where did these images come from if God is at some level unknowable? In the case of the major world religions, the answer to this question is divine revelation. It is a generally held belief in all religions that humans need to be helped to imagine what God is like. It is also believed that God reveals himself to people so that they can know and understand God better. This does not mean that human beings can ever know God fully, but they can strive to come closer to an understanding of the nature of God. The process whereby God discloses himself to humanity is known as **divine revelation**. Religious people believe that revelation begins with God who reveals himself to humanity through the human experience of the world, and it is up to human beings whether or not they respond to this revelation.

Revelation takes a number of forms:

- Universal or general revelation
- Particular, historical revelation

Universal revelation is where God makes himself known to all people at all times in all places. Through the wonder and beauty of creation, through our experience of the goodness and complexity of human beings, and through human experience in all its diversity, God is revealed. This type of divine revelation gives rise to basic religious faith. By this we mean a general belief that there is a transcendent being, present in the cosmos, who loves and cares for humanity. There is a more specific form of divine revelation, where God is believed to have revealed himself in a special way at a particular time and place. This type of divine revelation plays a central role in the three major monotheistic religions; it is known as **particular, historical revelation**. The Jewish, Christian and Islamic religions all believe that God revealed himself at particular moments in the history of the people of Israel.

Divine Revelation in Judaism

God revealed himself to the Jewish people throughout their history. Events such as the call of Abraham, the covenant with Yahweh, the Exodus experience and the covenant on Mount Sinai all marked moments when the people of Israel understood God as actively involving himself in their lives. These moments are key moments in the history of Judaism and as such contain laws recorded in the Hebrew Scriptures which are observed by the Jewish people. The **Decalogue,** or Ten Commandments, contains key elements of the Jewish faith. The practice of remembering God's saving presence in the observation of key festivals like **Passover** shows how the Jewish understanding of divine revelation affects religious practice.

This revelation of God, which began as an oral tradition, was later written down and became the Hebrew Scriptures. All three monotheistic religions are known as '**religions of the book**' because of their belief in historical revelation; that is, that God revealed himself to them in their history. However, the three have different understandings of divine revelation and these differences are reflected in the practices and rituals of the religions and the interpretation of the sacred texts.

For the Jewish people, the events recorded in scripture were of such significance that they responded in faith to this God who made himself known to them. The Jews of today still believe that God reveals himself in a general way through creation and human experience. But for them the Hebrew Scriptures are the most important source of God's self-revelation. They believe the scriptures to be the word of God. In Judaism, observance of the law and key religious festivals all have a scriptural basis.

from the Book of Kells

Divine Revelation in Christianity

Christians developed a different understanding of God's self-revelation because of the central role of Jesus Christ. While Christians believe in the Old Testament as a rich source of divine revelation, they believe that Jesus Christ is the high point of God's revelation to people. The life, death and resurrection of Jesus is understood by Christians as the climax and summation of God's involvement in history. The followers of Christ understand Jesus as God's most complete self-communication to humanity. The Vatican II document The Church in the Modern World states: 'The Lord Jesus Christ is the goal of human history, the focal point of the longings of history and civilisation, the centre of the human race, the joy of every heart and the answer to all its yearnings.'[36]

Christians believe that Jesus Christ is the Word made Flesh and as such is the definitive mediator between God and humanity. The promise of resurrection for all believers is a fundamental part of Christian faith. Tradition and the authority of the Christian community guide its members in interpreting God's self-revelation. For Christians, God was revealed in Jesus, but not completely; the final and ultimate revelation will occur in the future. Christians believe in a dynamic, ongoing revelation that will reach its fulfilment when Christ returns in glory at the end of time.

This belief in the ongoing nature of revelation has influenced the interpretation of scripture in the Christian tradition. The Christian sacrament of the Eucharist reflects this understanding of revelation and the central, unique role of Jesus Christ. In the Liturgy of the Eucharist the revelation of God in history is recognised in the reading from the Old Testament. The Gospel reading recognises the role of Jesus and his life, death and resurrection in divine revelation, which is ongoing. The liturgy of the Eucharist, in which the continued presence of Jesus is celebrated, is a key ritual for Christians.

Divine Revelation in Islam

Within Islam, there is another understanding of divine revelation. Muslims, like Jews and Christians, believe that God revealed himself to Abraham, Moses and the many prophets in the Hebrew

The Qur'an

Scriptures. However, Muslims believe that Jesus Christ was just one prophet among all the others. The Christian belief in the divinity of Jesus Christ is a concept utterly rejected by Muslims. They believe that Allah revealed himself for the last time in the sixth century. They believe that this revelation was the ultimate revelation, the complete and final guidance for humanity. This revelation is contained in the Qur'an, the sacred book of Islam. Muslims understand the Qur'an as the end of a long line of divine revelation from God to people through the prophets. This means that for Muslims the Qur'an is not open to change or criticism. The **five pillars of Islam** are the practices through which Muslims offer themselves fully to Allah. These practices have remained unchanged for centuries. Muslims believe them to be unchangeable because they are the will of Allah; there is nothing to be added to or taken from these pillars because they are faithful to the revelation given to Muhammad in the sixth century. For Muslims, the prophet Muhammad is the final and most important of all the prophets. The Qur'an is understood as the eternal word of God, God's great gift to them. It is treated with the greatest respect and reverence.

The Five Pillars of Islam are:

Shahadah – proclamation of the faith
Salat – ritual prayer five times a day
Zakat – duty to give alms
Sawn – fasting during Ramadan
Hajj – pilgrimage to Mecca

Questions

. What is meant by divine revelation?
. What are the 'religions of the book'?
. What is the most important source of divine revelation for Jews?
. What is the high point of divine revelation for Christians?
. What is the Muslim belief about divine revelation?
. What do you understand by the transcendent?
. Describe briefly how the transcendent is understood in two religious traditions.

Assignments

. Describe two forms of divine revelation.
. Write a note on the Christian understanding of divine revelation.
. Compare and contrast the distinct understanding of divine revelation in each of the three monotheistic world religions. Explain how this understanding influenced
a) religious practice.
b) the interpretation of religious texts in each of the three religions.

This topic is also considered in **Section C, World Religions**.

The Understanding of the Transcendent in two religious traditions

In the course of our search for meaning, it has become clear that some realities are beyond normal grasp or definition; in other words, they transcend the normal material reality. For example, how do you describe the beauty of a powerful song or piece of music or the (indescribable) love of a mother for a sick infant or the visceral effect of a sunset or sunrise at certain times in our lives? Religions then have difficulty describing a transcendent God. Christianity is unique in that it attempts to fuse the immanence and transcendence of God in the person of Jesus Christ. This is in contrast to the notion of the transcendent in Islam, where God is seen as absolute other, who communicates his will through the prophet Muhammad and the Qur'an.

In summary

● Divine revelation is the process whereby God discloses himself to humanity

● In the three monotheistic religions this divine revelation had an impact on religious practice and how these religions interpreted their sacred texts.

● Christianity and Islam have somewhat contrasting understandings of the transcendent.

Oral/Written Revision of Important Terms

Look up the following terms which you have come across in **bold** type in this chapter and briefly explain each one: **transcendent, divine revelation, universal revelation, historical revelation, Decalogue, Passover, religions of the book, Five Pillars of Islam.**

God said to
Moses, 'I am
who I am.'

(Exodus 3:14)

Chapter 7: Naming God, Past and Present

In this chapter you will learn about...

● the difficulty of describing a transcendent God

● traditional and contemporary images of God

● religious interpretations of contemporary human experience – prophetic, mystical, holy, poetic and aesthetic

● the 'proofs of God' from Anselm of Canterbury, Thomas Aquinas, Bonaventure, Isaac Newton

Group Work

Divide the class into groups of five students or less. Each group will need:
• one sheet of poster paper
• some crayons, colouring pencils or markers
• scissors, glue and magazines (*optional*)

Each group will depict graphically an image of God. Each member should think about their image of God first and then through group discussion agree on a group image that reflects the input of the group members.
Each group will be asked to present and explain their poster to the class.

When it comes to talking about God, we immediately run into difficulties. How do you describe with words what is beyond human language and beyond our full understanding? We use symbol and metaphor to try to describe our understanding of God. We can see how, from the beginning, humanity tried to speak of God, for example, God was like a father, a mother or a powerful leader, depending on the context.

Traditional and Contemporary Images of God

One of the most familiar **images of God** is 'father'. Jesus called God his father, even using the more intimate term 'abba'. In Luke 11:1-4 we read about the prayer Jesus taught his followers: 'Father, hallowed be your name.' The image of father represented the fact that God cared for humanity as a parent cares for his or her child. God would protect and guide his children.

Another image of God found in the Old Testament is that of 'Creator God'. In Genesis, God creates the world and humanity, and sees that it is good. God created humanity in his image: *'So God created humankind in his image, in the image of God he created them; male and female he created them'* (Genesis 1:27). This image links God to the beauty and diversity of the natural world. The image of God the creator expresses the belief that God existed before creation.

The image of God as 'all-powerful' is found in the Old Testament. '**Omnipotent**' means 'all powerful', and it is a quality that is attributed to God throughout history. This image arose during a time of great difficulty for the Jewish people. They needed a powerful God who would save them from slavery and oppression. This image of God expresses the belief that God looks after his people. Thus we see that the historical context affects the images used to describe God.

Today there are many different 'new' images of God, as well as the more traditional ones outlined above. One such image is that of God as 'mother'. In Isaiah 42:14 God is compared to a woman in labour, and in Isaiah 49:14-15 to a woman who cannot forget the

child she has borne. In the New Testament we find maternal images of God in Luke 13:20-21, where God is compared to a woman baking bread. Because of the cultural limitations of biblical times, when women had a secondary and subservient role in society, this image was not strong. However, in modern times, along with the social changes and progress, the feminine image is more acceptable. Many recognise the value and richness of the image of God as mother. This image expresses a belief in a loving, nurturing God. It also captures the creative dimension of God.

God as 'liberator' is an image that can be found in the Old Testament. We can see this in the call of Moses in Exodus 3:7-10. This image was rejuvenated with the birth of **liberation theology.** People who experienced oppression found the image of God as liberator empowering. This image reminds believers that God takes pity on the suffering and supports them in their struggle to live in a just world.

The image of God as 'love' is one that is familiar to many people. It is a modern image but it can also be found in the Bible. In Luke 15: 11-32 the story of the prodigal son contains the image of God as unconditional love. The experience of love and the desire for loving relationships make this image of God a powerful one. Love is an abstract concept, open to interpretation, and as such is a more open image for contemporary believers. This image expresses the unconditional love of God which, for Christians, is bound up with the life, death and resurrection of Jesus Christ.

Religious Interpretations of Contemporary Human Experience

The Prophetic interpretation

A **prophet** is a person who examines society and critiques it in the light of their religious beliefs. A prophetic stance is often one that challenges and critiques the status quo – the way things are – and cries out for change. The prophetic interpretation of human experience is a deeply religious one. Its roots are to be found in the Old Testament prophets, such as Amos, Jeremiah and Isaiah. We see it also in the New Testament with John the Baptist and Jesus himself. The prophet challenges people to change their behaviour, their attitudes and their lifestyle. This change is intended to create a world of greater justice for all. The prophet believes that behaviour that leads to injustice offends God and so it is the will of God that situations of injustice be corrected.

Because of the nature of the prophetic stance, prophets are often 'voices in the wilderness'. Many people resist any change that might affect their wealth and status within a society. This often results in the prophet being criticised, **marginalised** and sometimes ignored. The work of Fr Peter McVerry SJ is an excellent example of the prophetic stance in action. He has been described as one of the most prophetic voices in Ireland today.

Fr Peter McVerry

Fr McVerry is a Jesuit priest who has worked with homeless young people for many years. In 1974, as a newly ordained priest, he opted to live and work in Dublin's inner city, along with a small group of Jesuits. He began working with young people from severely disadvantaged families and communities. Many of these young people had left school early and were abusing drugs and alcohol. They had also become involved in crime and the future held little hope for them. What Peter McVerry saw through his work shocked and appalled him. However, the experience also challenged many of his own attitudes and opened his eyes to the divided society in which we live. Fr McVerry has continued to work in this field, questioning and

. What is meant by the prophetic interpretation of human experience?
. What attitudes are challenged by Peter McVerry?
. What does the extract from *The Meaning is in the Shadows* tell us about Peter McVerry's religious beliefs?
. Can you think of another example of a prophet in our world today?

Assignment

Look up the following biblical references and read the passages. Compare the passages and identify the message in each text. In what way are these texts prophetic?

  Isaiah 1:12-17
  Jeremiah 1:4-10
  Amos 3:1-8
  Mark 1:1- 5
  Luke 6:17-31

This topic is also considered in **Section F, Issues of Justice and Peace**.

challenging a society that tolerates such division and inequality. He is often heard on the media calling on Irish society to adopt a truly Christian response to the problem of poverty and deprivation. Justice, and therefore peace, will be attained only when those who call themselves followers of Jesus Christ live out the gospel values, which are both challenging and radical. In his book, *The Meaning is in the Shadows*, Peter McVerry describes the life of three young men, Donal, Frank and John:

Like Frank, homeless, in the care of the Health Board, who had been accessing accommodation on a nightly basis from the emergency overnight social work service. On the night of his eighteenth birthday, he went, as usual, to the emergency service, only to be told that since he was now eighteen he was no longer eligible for the service. He 'celebrated' the night of his eighteenth birthday in a doorway. He is still on the streets. Adulthood in the shadows.

Everyone was too busy making money, too busy spending money, to notice John and Frank and Donal suffering in the shadows. And the politicians were too busy helping everyone to make even more money, and helping everyone to spend even more money, to notice John and Frank and Donal in the shadows. Most of those in the shadows are unaware that they are, in fact, God's favourites; that Jesus too came and lived in the shadows. He too experienced the rejection, the misunderstanding and the suffering imposed (or not taken away) for reasons of political expediency. God became one of them.

And most of us, as we rush to work, to play or to spend, and seek to find security for our children in our assets and bank balances, sometimes we pause to try and find meaning in it all. The hassle, the stress, the rush – what is it all for?

We search here, we search there, but we cannot find an answer that satisfies our deeper selves. We look deep into ourselves, we look up at the sky, we look to the East (no point in looking to the West), but the meaning of all this frantic activity eludes us.

Of course it does because the meaning is in the shadows.[37]

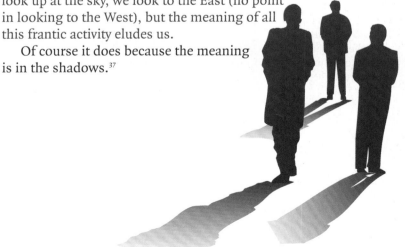

1. Can you explain and give an example of the mystical interpretation of human experience?
2. In what way is the mystical interpretation of experience different from the prophetic?
3. Mystical practices have become very popular in recent years. Why do you think this is so?
4. What mystical practices are most popular with Catholics? Have you experienced any of these?

Assignment

Research what life is like in a contemplative order, such as the Cistercians, the Trappists, the Benedictines and the Carmelites. Find out the following:
- where these orders are located in Ireland;
- what life is like for a member of the order;
- the core values of this way of life;
- why these orders continue to flourish and attract vocations.

The Mystical interpretation

Eat Your Own Fruit
A disciple once complained, 'You tell us stories,
but you never reveal their meaning to us.'
Said the master, 'How would you like it if
someone offered you fruit and masticated
[chewed] it before giving it to you?'
No one can find your meaning for you.
Not even the master.
(Anthony De Mello)[38]

Unlike the prophetic interpretation of human experience, the mystical interpretation does not seek to challenge society or critique behaviour. The **mystical interpretation** of experience seek to make an inner journey and leave behind the distractions of the world. This interpretation of life is found in all faiths. The individual seeks to know God, or the transcendent, in a personal and intense way. The mystical journey involves the imagination rather than logic. Through meditation, prayer and contemplation, the person may experience God. The mystical interpretation of human experience has become very popular in recent times. Perhaps this can be explained by the dramatic increase in the pace of life, along with the growing materialism of the world in which we live. Many people would say that the return to the mystical is a reaction to the pressures of modern life. More and more people

Questions

1. What is meant by a holy or sacred interpretation of life?
2. Can you give some examples of what could be called sacred moments in the lives of people today?
3. Can you recall a sacred moment in your own life and the effect that had on you?

realise that wealth and beauty do not guarantee happiness, and so people are looking elsewhere. Mystical practices offer an alternative means of fulfilment.

Buddhism is an example of a mystical interpretation of life. It is a belief system that places great emphasis on the importance of meditation. Buddhists believe that life is constantly changing and that happiness is not to be found in the things of this life, such as wealth, possessions, beauty or fame, as all of these things will disappear. Rather, it is by freeing ourselves from these things that we will achieve enlightenment. For Buddhists, this state of enlightenment is called *nirvana*. Buddhism strives to encourage people to take time out to meditate on the deeper, more spiritual side of human existence.

The mystical approach to life is common to all faiths. Christians may use meditation and contemplative prayer as a means of experiencing God in a personal way. This mystical experience sustains them in their daily lives.

The Holy Interpretation

Another example of a religious interpretation of human experience is the '**holy**'. The religious rituals of today have their roots in the past. To interpret human experience as holy means to understand events in our lives as sacred. Birth, death, marriage and life choices are seen as events in which God is present. When life is seen as holy, then special times are celebrated through ritual and prayer. The joys and sorrows of life are understood to be holy.

Within Christianity, the sacraments are examples of the holy interpretation of experience. Baptism celebrates the arrival of a new member into the Christian community; the ritual is rich in symbolism, from the water of new life to the white robes signifying a new life in Christ. The funeral rite reveals an understanding of death as the beginning of new life in Christ; the ritual seeks to comfort those who grieve, but also recognises the hope in the resurrection. The joyful experience of falling in love and the decision to commit oneself to another is interpreted by many as holy. The celebration of marriage in the Church recognises the sacredness of the covenant of marriage. This ritual brings together the couple, their family and friends in the presence of God and recognises that it is holy.

This topic is also considered in **Section G, Worship, Prayer and Ritual** and **Section H, The Bible: Literature and Sacred Text**.

The Poetic and Aesthetic interpretation

People who are artistic and creative often choose to express their

religious interpretation of life through poetry, music and art. For many, great beauty suggests the presence of God. Some people are inspired to create poems, paintings, music and sculpture as a way of expressing their religious beliefs. The **poetic and aesthetic** interpretation of experience is a source of inspiration for all. The writer John Shea has written poetry that is deeply religious but connected to everyday life. One of his poems, taken from the collection *The Hour of the Unexpected*, is entitled 'A Prayer to the God who will not go away':

Lord,
you are the poetry of wordless lives,
the salting of tasteless purposes,
the reminder that we are more than
the sinking spiral of the dying sparrow
and that the reckless rush of the galaxies
marvel at the human collision of a kiss.
You are the tightening hope
that someone has stretched a net
beneath this high wire act of ours.[39]

Here Shea expresses his belief that it is God who gives purpose and meaning to our lives. He also celebrates his faith in the presence of a Being who protects and cares for us. John O'Donohue, an Irish poet and scholar, is another example of someone who expresses his religious interpretation of life today through literature. Through his aesthetic use of language he offers the reader an inspiring and religious way in which to understand human experience and contemporary issues. His book *Anam Cara* is full of spiritual wisdom from the Celtic world through which he explores topics such as friendship, work, ageing and death. The following is a brief extract:

1. What is meant by the poetic or aesthetic interpretation of life?
2. How does poetry lend itself to the expression of religious belief?
3. Isolate what you think is the central theme in John Shea's or John O'Donoghue's poem and explain it in your own words.
4. Is there any other poem or piece of music that captures religious belief for you?

The Dead Bless Us

I feel that our friends amongst the dead
really mind us and look out for us.
Often there might be a big boulder of misery
over your path about to fall on you,
but your friends amongst the dead hold it
back until you have passed by.
We do not need to grieve for the dead.
Why should we grieve for them?

They are now in a place where there is no
more shadow, darkness, loneliness,
isolation or pain. They are home.
They are with God from
whom they came.
They have returned to
the nest of their identity
within the great circle of
God.
God is the greatest circle
of all, the largest embrace in the
universe which holds
visible and invisible, temporal and
eternal as one.[40]

Proofs of God
(Higher Level)

St Anselm

The scholastic philosopher and
theologian Anselm of Canterbury
(1033-1109) was born at Aosta in
Piedmont. He was Archbishop of
Canterbury from 1093 to 1109.
Anselm was one of the first
medievals to try to prove that God
existed and he is sometimes
therefore referred to as the
father of scholasticism. He
began with the belief in the
existence of God. For
Anselm, this was not just a
question of faith. He
believed that our
existence meant that
there must necessarily

exist a more perfect being. Anselm said that God was something that was greater than anything else one could think of or conceive. For Anselm:

● The term 'God' refers to the greatest conceivable being.
● Real existence (existence in reality) is greater than mere existence in the understanding.
● Therefore, God must exist in reality, not just in the understanding.

If God existed in the mind only and not in reality, God would not be the greatest being conceivable. Since the time of Immanuel Kant, this has been known as the **ontological argument** for the existence of God. To the modern reader and thinker, this may seem implausible; however, there is a definite logic to this argument.

St Thomas Aquinas

Anselm was not the only thinker to devise proofs for the existence of God. St Thomas Aquinas (1225-74), whom we read about in chapter 2, belonged to an era in which reason was much admired. In an effort to make faith a reasonable subject of discussion, he composed five **proofs for the existence of God**:

1. The existence of a **prime mover** (as in life-giver) – nothing can move itself; there must be a first mover. This first mover is called God.
2. Cause of existence – things that exist are created by other things; nothing can create itself. There must be, at the beginning, an **uncreated creator**, called God. God is the first cause.
3. The existence of a **necessary Being**, which causes the existence of others. This necessary Being is called God.
4. Degrees of perfection – for any given quality (e.g. beauty, goodness) there must be a **perfect standard** by which all such qualities are measured. This perfect standard is called God.
5. Intelligent design – we can see that the universe works and is ordered, thus we can conclude that it was designed by an **intelligent designer.** We call this intelligent designer God.

To appreciate what these theologians were trying to do, we need to remember the context in which they were working. They wanted to argue that faith, and particularly faith in God, was rational and could be defended in the philosophical climate of the day. Each generation would face the task of explaining the idea and experience of God.

St Bonaventure

Bonaventure, a contemporary of Aquinas, sought to prove the

existence of God in a slightly different way. Bonaventure, a Franciscan, drew on the life of St Francis, the founder of the Franciscans, in his writings on this issue. In his book, *The Journey of the Mind to God*, he combined the philosophical approach, the use of reason and logic, with religious experience. He emphasised the importance of spiritual experience in understanding God. Bonaventure believed that by looking at the life of St Francis you could find evidence for the existence of God.

In reaching this conclusion, he used Anselm's proof for the existence of God. According to Bonaventure, St Francis had achieved an excellence in his life that appeared to be beyond what was human. This suggested that it was possible for human beings to '...*see and understand that the "best" is... that than which nothing better can be imagined*'.[41] The very fact that we could imagine the 'best' meant that it must exist in the perfection of God. This understanding of God involved an inner journey on the part of the believer. The believer must look into the self, where he or she would be '...*transported in ecstasy above the intellect and find a vision of God that transcended our limited notions...*'.[42]

This method of 'proof' was not intended to convince unbelievers. Bonaventure saw religious experience as a necessary part of this 'proof'.

Isaac Newton

History has recorded the different attempts to understand and 'prove' the existence of God. The seventeenth century is no exception. The Enlightenment produced writers in all areas, none more so than in science. Isaac Newton (1642-1727), the English physicist, was a scientist first and foremost. However, in his efforts to describe the physical universe, he understood God as an essential part of the system. Newton was convinced that when he thought about the universe, he could prove the existence of God. He asked the question: why had the internal gravity present in the universe not pulled all the planets and systems together into one big mass? He concluded that this did not happen because they had been carefully

1. What do you understand by 'proofs of God'?
2. Summarise briefly St Anselm's argument for the existence of God.
3. What were St Thomas Aquinas' five proofs?
4. What contribution did St Bonaventure and Isaac Newton make to this debate?

Assignment

Write a brief note on the traditional proofs of God in the writings of one of the following:
   Anselm
   Aquinas
   Bonaventure
   Newton

Class Debate

Prepare a class debate on the issue of the existence of God. Divide into two teams. One team should argue for the existence of God, while the other could argue that it is not possible to prove the existence of God.

placed in their positions. This pointed to an intelligent, powerful Being who governed the movement of individual planets and the entire system so that life was possible. The Being who oversaw all of this perfection in the universe must indeed be a perfect intelligence.

In *The Principals of Natural Philosophy* (1687) Newton wrote:

'This most beautiful system of the sun, planets and comets could only proceed from the counsel and dominion of an intelligent and powerful Being.'[43]

In summary

- Describing a transcendent God is difficult for finite humans.
- There are many traditional and contemporary images of God.
- Some philosophers and theologians have attempted to provide rational explanation for the existence of God, among them St Anselm, St Thomas Aquinas, St Bonaventure, and Isaac Newton.

Oral/Written Revision of Important Terms

Look up the following terms which you have come across in **bold** type in this chapter and briefly explain each one: **images of God, omnipotent, liberation theology, prophet, marginalised, mystical interpretation, holy, poetic and aesthetic, ontological argument, proofs for the existence of God, 'prime mover', 'uncreated creator', 'a necessary Being', 'perfect standard', 'intelligent designer'.**

Part Four: Religion and the Emergence of Values

I can only answer the question, 'What am I to do?', if I can answer the prior question, 'Of what story or stories do I find myself a part?'

(Alasdair MacIntyre)

In this chapter you will learn about...

● how the understanding of God affects the understanding of the person in the major religions of the world.

● how the understanding of the person in the religious traditions of Judaism, Christianity and Islam impacts on people's behaviour.

The title of this book presupposes that there are such things as meaning and values and, furthermore, that human beings have searched for both from the beginning. The previous chapters have examined the idea that this search for meaning is part of what it means to be a human being; in other words, it is part of our nature. We have looked at expressions of this search in contemporary culture and in ancient cultures. The worlds of myth, philosophy and science have all contributed to this quest. Religion seeks to answer the questions of life from a particular perspective. In the previous chapter we explored the concept of God as it emerged in human history. An understanding of God and God's relationship with human beings is central to a religious response to the great questions of life. It is to this issue that we now turn.

How does our understanding of God influence
● our self-understanding?
● our understanding of our world?

From a religious perspective, the quest for meaning and values is understood as a quest that leads us into the realm of the sacred or transcendent.

Religion in general is a source of symbols and rituals which enable people to name key moments and events. Religion encourages people to gather together and to discover the meaning and values by which to live. Each religion has a particular focus, set of rituals and set of beliefs; however, all of them have in common a belief in God or a divine being. This belief is central to how each religion responds to the key questions of life.

This topic is also considered in **Section D, Moral Decision-Making**.

Religion as a Source of Communal Values

The three major monotheistic world religions are Christianity, Judaism and Islam. These religions have a long history and the largest number of followers. There are many other important religions, but for our purposes here we will consider these three. The **concept of God** is distinct in each of these religions. In each, the particular understanding of God and God's relationship with humanity has resulted in a different understanding of the individual and of what constitutes right living. It would be far beyond the scope of this book to examine all the images of God within these religions, so we will concentrate on a central image or concept in each tradition and examine how it has affected the understanding of the person.

God and the Person in Judaism

'So God created humankind in his image,
in the image of God he created them,
male and female he created them.' (Genesis 1:27)

In seeking to understand the concepts of God in Judaism, we will look at the creation accounts in the Hebrew Scriptures and at the story of the Exodus of the Jewish people from Egypt. Each of these is significant in terms of the concept of God and its effect on Judaism. However, it's important to remember that they are not the only sources of information on the Jewish understanding of God in creation. The Psalms, the book of Proverbs, the books of the prophets and the book of Job, among others, also throw light on this issue.

The Wailing Wall in Jerusalem

There are two accounts of creation in the book of Genesis. The first account is in Genesis 1:1 to Genesis 2:3. This account tells of the

seven days of creation, culminating in the seventh day, on which God rested. The making of humanity by God occurs on the sixth day. God created humanity in the divine image. Out of all that was created, all life on earth, humanity was unique in its likeness to the divine creator. This account of creation was written at a time when the people of Israel were suffering exile in Babylon. They may have begun to feel abandoned by their God and in despair about their future. This creation account reminds them that God is powerful. God created order and light out of chaos and darkness. More importantly still, God created humanity, and humanity is in relationship with God. Surely this God would not abandon them!

The second account of creation is actually much older than the first one. It occurs in Genesis 2:4 to Genesis 3:24. Scholars agree that the purpose here is not to give a historical account of the details or sequence of creation but to remind people of their relationship to God. This account details both the creation of humanity, in which male and female are equal, and the 'fall', where humanity becomes estranged from God. This paradoxical situation of being created and loved by God and also being estranged from God has an influence on the self-understanding of believers. The God of these creation accounts is outside of creation but involved in it. This God was involved in the beginning and continues to be involved in the ongoing creation of Israel. In the eyes of God, creation is good. There is a special and intimate relationship between God and humanity. Alongside this special relationship there is an experience of distance from God. One of the dominant themes of the Hebrew Scriptures is that nobody has ever seen the face of God. The reason for this may be the belief that humanity is incapable of understanding the wonder of God. It is also possible that this is related to the initial estrangement. Humanity is not worthy, because of sin, to see the face of God. One of the consequences of this concept of God was the prohibition against the worship of images or idols. Judaism is a monotheistic religion. Combined with the belief that no one could see the face of God, you have a strict rule about the worship of idols. The Hebrew Scriptures are rich in references to this issue.

The God that is revealed in the Exodus accounts is a powerful God but one who feels pity and hears the cry of the people in exile. God is revealed as a liberating God in the Exodus event. This event became the central event in the Jewish celebration of the Passover. God was a faithful God who fulfilled promises and expected the same in return. The idea of **covenant** is at the heart of Judaism. It expresses a unique bond between God and people. It is built on past deeds but is committed to future relationship. From the covenant agreement emerges a strong adherence to the Law as outlined in the scriptures. The image of God as lawgiver results in a tremendous respect for the Law in every detail. The concept of God in Judaism is closely linked to the idea of covenant. God called the people of Israel; through Moses God led them out of slavery and into the

Assignments

1. Write a brief note on the understanding of God in Judaism. Refer to the creation accounts, the Exodus event and the idea of covenant.
2. Explain how the concept of God affected the understanding of the person in Judaism? Refer to the creation of humanity, the place of the law, and worship.

Promised Land. As part of the covenant the Jewish people remained faithful to the Law and in their worship they remembered their liberation. We can see in this brief analysis how the concept of God affected and influenced the behaviour of Jews. In their fidelity to the Law, their attitude to the land of Israel and their worship, we can see how the relationship between God and the person in Judaism has affected the people's daily lives.

God and the Person in Christianity

Christianity draws on the same creation accounts as those of Judaism. The Old Testament of the Christian Bible contains many of the books sacred to Judaism. Indeed, the two religions share a common heritage. For Christians, the Creator God of Genesis is the same God who is revealed through Jesus in the New Testament. The creation accounts reveal that God is the creator of the universe. Christianity has focused on the activity of creation and the fact that a distinction must be made between God and creation. In Christianity, God is not equal to creation. However, because God created the world in all its beauty and diversity, Christianity advocates a spirituality that holds all that God created in high regard. Such a world-affirming spirituality can be seen in early Christian writings. Creation can be good, but no aspect of it, whether person, place or institution, can ever be seen as divine.

Within the Christian understanding of creation, humanity is given the special task of caring for creation. This idea of human **stewardship** has important consequences for our treatment of the earth. Because human beings have a special role and relationship with God, they are expected to care for the earth. The creation is not ours but is entrusted to us by God. We may be the high point of creation but we have been given this responsibility. The ecological and environmental implications of this concept are rich indeed. If it matters to God how we treat the earth, then we can see how failure to do so could be understood as sinful.

The creation accounts are important for how we understand ourselves and our place within creation. God created human beings with the intention that they should be in relationship with God. Within Christianity, this relationship is fundamental. Without it, humanity will not reach its true potential; 'You made us for yourself, and our hearts are restless until they find their rest in you' (Augustine of Hippo). The God in the creation accounts is a loving God who created a world of beauty and placed it in the care of humanity. The creation of humanity by God and God's love for humanity means that Christians everywhere are called to recognise the sacredness of human life.

In Christianity, God is revealed in a unique way through Jesus Christ. God, who thus far had been invisible, is made visible and known through Jesus. The life, death and resurrection of Jesus are the foundational events of Christianity. The belief that God became part of human history in the person of Jesus is known as the doctrine of the **Incarnation**. The Incarnation is central to the Christian understanding of God and humanity. Colossians 1:15 tells us that Jesus is 'the image of the invisible God'.

In John 14:9 we read: 'Whoever has seen me has seen the Father.' Through Jesus, humanity was forgiven and redeemed. The death and resurrection of Jesus revealed God's unconditional love for humanity. The life of Jesus shows the followers of Christ how to live. Jesus lived and preached of a world where mercy ruled justice, where the despised were loved and where love of God was the centre of one's life. Through his life and teaching he called on people to choose peace over violence, to include rather than exclude, and to share rather than hoard. All of this he based on the understanding of God as loving, forgiving and involved in the world. One of the most fundamental implications of this understanding of God for Christians is that in all areas of life they are called to live as Christ did. The revelation of God in Christ is at the heart of the Church's mission. The Church must mediate the ongoing revelation of God through the Holy Spirit to humanity. The mission of the Church is 'to reveal the mystery of God, who is the ultimate goal of [the human person].'[44]

Assignments

1. Write a note on the understanding of God in Christianity. Refer to the creation of the earth, the creation of humanity, and Jesus Christ.
2. Write a short note (about three paragraphs) on how the concept of God in Christianity affected the idea of the person and what was expected of them. Refer to stewardship, the sacredness of human life, and the doctrine of the Incarnation.
3. Read Luke 6:17-31. What are the implications for Christians who would follow Jesus?

God and the Person in Islam

The word Islam is Arabic and means 'peace' and 'submission'. Islam may be described as '...*a commitment to surrender one's will to the Will of God*'.[45] This central belief and attitude has direct consequences for the life of a Muslim.

Muslims believe that the word of God was passed down through the prophets, beginning with Adam and ending with Muhammad. Moses and Jesus are regarded as holy prophets, but the final and most important prophet was Muhammad. The Qur'an is the central book of Islam as it is believed to contain the word of God. The Qur'an and the life of Muhammad constitute the centre of Islamic faith.

The key belief in Islam is contained in the **Shahadah**, the first part of which is 'LA ILAHA ILLA ALLAH'. Translated, this means 'There is no god but The God'. The 'oneness' of God is central to Islam. In its strict monotheism, Islam is similar to both Judaism and Christianity. This belief has implications for Muslims in their worship and their daily lives. There are strict rules against polytheism or raising anything or anyone to the level of a god.

The term most frequently used about God in the Qur'an is 'merciful'. As is the case in Judaism and Christianity, the Qur'an reminds people that creation is a sign of God's existence and generosity. In Islam, God the creator is merciful and has provided for all people. In the Qur'an there are many reminders to people that they were created by God and should therefore respond with reverence and gratitude. This attitude should pervade all of life and lead to the transformation of the world, where God is worshipped in praise and thanks. The duty of worship comes from the understanding of God as the One, all-powerful and merciful. The submission of one's will to God is also evident in Islamic worship.

1. Write a brief note on the concept of God in Islam. Pay particular attention to the meaning of Islam, the 'oneness' of God, and the merciful nature of God.
2. Write a note on how the concept of God in Islam has a direct effect on the understanding of the person in that religion and has led to specific practices among Muslims.

Salat is the term that refers to the ritual prayer of Islam. It is one of the five pillars of Islam. This ritual prayer was central to Islam from the beginning. Salat requires that a Muslim prays five times a day: as dawn is breaking, in early afternoon, late afternoon, immediately after sunset, and any time after darkness has fallen. At the call to prayer, Muslims are invited to cease whatever they are doing and prepare for prayer. This preparation involves ritually purifying oneself. The worshipper may use a prayer mat when praying and will always face in the direction of Mecca, the holy city of Islam. The salat is always prayed in Arabic. It is profoundly symbolic of Muslim religious attitudes and expresses the core beliefs of Islam; that is, surrender in worship and obedience to the One God. The Qur'an contains the word of God as it passed from God to Muhammad. It includes an account of Muhammad's own experience of divine mercy.

The Qur'an warns against arrogance and selfishness. From this comes a strong emphasis on the need to help the poor and weak of the community. This principle of faith can be seen in the concrete obligation of **zakat**. Zakat is one of the five pillars of Islam and refers to the duty to give a proportion of one's wealth to the needy in your community. This religious duty of almsgiving is one that all Muslims must undertake. The Qur'an insists that those who have are obliged to help those who have not. This obligation has the double effect of helping the needy while also serving as an act of gratitude for one's own wealth and prosperity.

In looking at just two of the five pillars of Islam, we can see how the understanding of God in Islam has a direct and profound effect on how Muslims live their lives. As with Judaism and Christianity, Islam is organised around a holy book, which is believed to be the word of God.

In summary

- How we understand God has a bearing on how we understand the person in all the major world religions.
- In Judaism there is a special and intimate relationship between God and humanity, expressed in the covenant.
- The Incarnation is the foundational event for Christians.
- Islam requires a submission of one's will to the will of God.
- How these religions understand the person has an impact on human behaviour.

Oral/Written Revision of Important Terms

Look up the following terms which you have come across in **bold** type in this chapter and briefly explain each one: **concept of God, covenant, stewardship, incarnation, Shahadah, salat, zakat.**

In the time of innocence I did not know that morality existed. I know it now.

(Albert Camus)

In this chapter you will learn about...

● three key moments in the emergence of a secular world

● how values emerge from sources other than religious sources

● how religion relates to secular culture

Earlier in this text (chapter 4) we noted that the religious response to the great questions of life is not the only response. While all cultures, without exception, trace their roots back to a mythic/religious world view, this world view has been challenged by other ways of approaching life's ultimate questions. The word '**secular**' refers to a 'this-worldly' way of understanding human existence. It is the opposite of religious and as a world view it does not make any reference to the existence of a god or the 'sacred' in human life. In modern culture there are a variety of world views from which certain values have emerged. In turn, these values have shaped the communities and cultures from which they emerged. In some cases these world views are in opposition to a religious world view. In other cases there is a certain degree of harmony. In the previous section we looked at how some of the world religions seek to define values for their followers. Now we will examine some of the important moments in the development of a non-religious world view and the values that emerged from these philosophies.

The Renaissance

A religious view has an 'other-worldly' focus and maintains a belief in

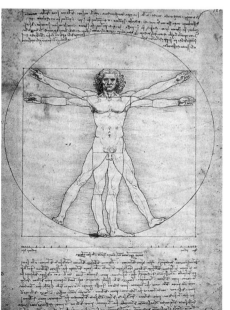

God. Secularisation refers to the process by which a culture defines itself in a 'this-worldly' context.[46] As a result of secularisation, the world view of **secularism** developed. Secularism places the person at the centre of everything and values the human ability to reason above all else. Secularism can be traced back to the Renaissance in the fifteenth and sixteenth centuries. As we have seen, the **Renaissance** was a period of tremendous energy and upheaval. It began in Italy and gradually moved throughout Europe. The Renaissance refers to changes and innovation in a wide variety of disciplines – art, music, literature, architecture, economics, philosophy and religion. In the context of understanding secular sources of values that influenced society, it is the emergence of humanism that is of interest to us.

In chapter 4 we saw that humanism is a philosophy or world view that says there is nothing higher or other than human existence. Renaissance humanism was characterised by individualism; it placed the person at the centre. Each individual was seen as unique and special and as potentially having the ability to understand the world. This world view valued the power of reason and the uniqueness of the person above all else. Today we can see this emphasis on the individual throughout our society.

This confidence in human potential and the belief in the power of human reason led to enormous creativity in all areas of human life. It is in the area of scientific discovery that we can see the most outstanding achievements. The growth of scientific reasoning and skills can be linked to the emergence of secular humanism in the Renaissance. Modern scientific discoveries can also be traced back to this period in human history.

Assignment

Write a note on the development of secularism at the time of the Renaissance.

The Enlightenment

You may recall that the Enlightenment refers to a period in history in which a group of thinkers in Europe proposed a new way of viewing the world. As with the Renaissance, the theories of this period influenced the way in which society found meaning and created values. The Enlightenment took place mainly in the eighteenth century, when philosophers in England, Ireland, France and Germany began to create a particular world view in response to the social and political situation in Europe at that time. These thinkers sought to break free from what they saw as the immature position of blind faith in the Church and other authorities. The Enlightenment philosophers believed that it was humankind itself, through reason, that determined how life should be organised.

The motto of the Enlightenment could be summed up as 'Have the courage to know'. The most intense and important period of the Enlightenment was between the English Revolution in 1688 and the French Revolution in 1789. All over Europe people were becoming more aware of developments in science and philosophy. This era saw the birth of the 'coffee-house' as a place where people could meet and share opinions on many subjects. There was a dramatic increase in publications like pamphlets and literary magazines, which contributed to the growth of open debate and thought. During this period there emerged new forms of literature and drama. One important feature of this time was the breaking down of class barriers. In the coffee-houses and salons of Europe it became fashionable to ignore differences in social status. This was in contrast to the Court of the King, for example, where only the nobility were permitted to attend. Out of this period there emerged what was to become the motto of the French Revolution: '**Liberty, Equality and Fraternity.**' These aims came to be seen as rights, more specifically as human rights. The idea of human rights,

which is so familiar to the modern reader, took shape in this period. Towards the end of the eighteenth century, Thomas Paine, the best known political writer of his day, who was actively involved in the American Revolution (1773-83) and the French Revolution (1789-92), wrote two books: *The Age of Reason* and *The Rights of Man*. The first title can be used as a description of the century as a whole, while the second states one of the major themes of this period.[47] In 1789 the National Assembly of France approved the *Declaration on the Rights of Man and the Citizen*. This document was to become the model for much of Europe and indeed for the Constitution of the United States of America. The introduction to the Declaration lays out the rationale behind it:

> The representatives of the French people, organised as a National Assembly, believing that the ignorance, neglect, or contempt of the rights of man are the sole cause of public calamities and of the corruption of governments, have determined to set forth in a solemn declaration the natural, unalienable, and sacred rights of man, in order that this declaration, being constantly before all members of the Social body, shall remind them continually of their rights and duties.[48]

This document contains a list of seventeen 'rights' considered by its authors to be essential to the happiness of all. The first right stated: **Men are born and remain free and equal in rights. Social distinctions may be founded only on the general good.**[49]

This first article can be compared to the first article of the *Universal Declaration of Human Rights* passed by the United Nations after the First World War. We can see the continuation of the humanism of the Enlightenment in the world view and values expressed by the United Nations in their declaration. The *Declaration on the Rights of Man and the Citizen* is one of the founding documents in the human rights tradition. It grew out of a particular set of circumstances and the philosophical culture of the Enlightenment, where 'reason' and 'liberty' came together.

Assignment

Write a note on the 'rights of man' as they evolved from the period of the Enlightenment.

Existentialism – the philosophy of the twentieth century

One of the most influential philosophies of the twentieth century was existentialism. (You may recall the founder of existentialism who was mentioned in chapter 2) The beginning of the twentieth century was marked by the First World War. This terrible event saw millions die and massive casualties. As its name implies, it was the first time the world had witnessed such carnage and violence. The impact on the new generation cannot be underestimated. Many were disillusioned and no longer cared for the values of the previous generation. They did not look to the Church for meaning. Instead, they believed that in the quest for meaning the person had nothing more than themselves. The spirit of the age was marked by discontent. The fact that one existed in the world was the starting point in this philosophy. The freedom to choose one's own life and the dangers of making the wrong choice are the central concerns of the existentialist philosophers. One such philosopher was Jean-Paul Sartre.

Jean-Paul Sartre (1905-80)

Sartre was a prominent figure in French politics and public life in the 1960s. He is considered to be the proponent of existentialism as a world view. 'Man is condemned to be free' is one of his most famous pronouncements. This reveals some of the values that come from existentialism. The person is solely responsible for their own life.

There is no meaning to be found. Human life cannot be given any meaning from the outside. This world view was bleak and unrelenting in its insistence that all anyone had was the fact of their existence. However, another element of Sartre's philosophy was that the person is called to take up the fact of his/her existence, to make a commitment to life and to take full responsibility for that decision. This seems like a contradiction; if there is no meaning, why bother? According to an existentialist world view, each person is responsible for the choices they make, and each human being must decide for or against a particular course of action and take responsibility for that decision. In an existentialist world view, there are no criteria for deciding what are the right decisions and the wrong decisions. Existentialism rejects the possibility of meaning being found outside the person and is characterised by the complete rejection of all other meanings that are on offer. The philosophy of existentialism made an important contribution to secular humanism as it exists today. With its emphasis on the individual and the distrust of any 'meaning' offered from other sources, like religion, it has had an enormous impact on the values of contemporary Western societies.

Assignment

Write a note on the important contribution that existentialism has made to secular humanism as it exists today.

Secular Sources of Communal Values

Over the course of this book we have been looking at the many ways in which human beings have tried to find answers to the big questions of life. It is clear that these questions have been asked many times throughout human history. We looked at the mythical response to the search for meaning and values, and at the philosophical developments that followed. Permeating these two ways of responding to the search for meaning was the religious response. We have also seen how a secular or non-religious response to the search for meaning developed in human history.

All of these ways of understanding our universe and our place within it coexist today. A religious world view finds meaning and value through faith in the divine and transcendent – God. A secular world view does not look for meaning outside of the person, but yet it has given rise to values that are important and may also be found in the religious world view, values such as the equality of all people, the dignity of human life, tolerance and compassion. However, there are other values that have emerged from a secular world view that are at odds with some religious convictions and values.

Class Activity

Examine the following list of values.

What do you value?

- Self-sufficiency
- Freedom
- Equality
- Kindness
- Patience
- Inner peace
- Humility
- Self-control
- Faith in God
- Good health
- Wealth
- Happy family
- Being found attractive
- Loving
- Trust
- Physical fitness
- Happiness
- Maturity
- National identity
- Respect for others
- Security
- Self-respect
- Sense of accomplishment
- Friendship
- Understanding of myself and my place in the world
- Being a good student

1. Which of the above values would you consider to be religious values?
2. Which ones would you consider to be non-religious (secular)?
3. Name the values that you consider are common to both secular and religious world views.
4. Choose four values from the list that are most important to you. You may add any value that is important to you that is not already listed.
5. Having considered these values, can you think of any secular organisations or movements that work for these values in our society?

We will now examine secular sources of values that have influenced our society today.

The feminist movement

As we have seen, the Enlightenment gave rise to a period of great change for artists, those in education, philosophy and science, and writers of all kinds. Humanism emerged from this period and there was a renewed sense of human potential. Ideas such as tolerance, equality, natural rights and education rights flourished in the period before the French Revolution. Within this broad context we can find the beginnings of some specific movements. One of these movements was the women's movement or **feminism.**

The beginnings of modern feminism can be traced to the period around the French Revolution. Women were involved at all levels of this tremendous upheaval. However, when it came to the *Declaration on the Rights of Man and the Citizen*, only men were considered citizens. Women were active in the revolution, as they were in all modern revolutions to follow; yet again and again the cause of equality was ignored or overlooked in the battles for liberation. Olympe de Gouges (1748-93) composed the *Declaration on the Rights of Woman and the Female Citizen* in 1791. In this declaration she called for better education rights and equal rights within marriage for women. In this climate others were inspired to seek equal rights for women. In England, Mary Wollstonecraft (1759-97) published her *Vindications of the Rights of Women* in 1792. However, in 1793 all women were barred from political activity in France and Olympe de Gouges was guillotined. The revolution did not include equality for women!

The First World War changed the lives of everyone in Europe and beyond. Indeed, this event changed the world. The lives of women were dramatically altered because of the war. Women found themselves taking up roles that hitherto had been the preserve of men, and they did so with energy and courage. After the war the struggle to allow women to vote was over in many countries. Feminism is a broad term that includes many different strands, depending on the times in which it flourishes. However, its concern for the quality of life for families, for women, men

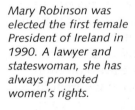

Mary Robinson was elected the first female President of Ireland in 1990. A lawyer and stateswoman, she has always promoted women's rights.

This topic is also considered in **Section I, Religion: The Irish Experience**.

and children in the world unites many of these strands. Feminism brought the values of equality to the political, social and personal arenas of life. As a movement it promoted the value of one's lived experience when making a judgement. It allowed women to speak about their lives in a way that was unheard of up to the beginning of the twentieth century. The voices of women needed to be heard in the places where laws were made; laws about marriage, inheritance, property, political involvement, child care, child labour, etc. These areas needed to change for all members of society. Without those who collected and remembered the stories of women throughout history, 'feminism' would not exist. Today women and men continue to seek equality in the areas of pay, employment and political representation. The issues of child care and access to education are areas that affect many people, both women and men. We in Ireland and Europe have equality legislation that provides protection for all members of society. Feminism was one of the movements that led to such legislation.

The family

When we are thinking about where values come from, we need look no further than our family. Our **family** teaches us values in both explicit and implicit ways. By this we mean that our parents or guardians *tell us* that some things or behaviours are 'good' or 'bad' (explicit), but we also learn from what we *see and experience* in our family (implicit). Sometimes the values can be conflicting. For example, if a parent slaps a child as a punishment for slapping another, then you can see that implicit and explicit values are contradictory. Experts tell us that we learn far more from what we experience and see than from what we are told. The family may not be a 'secular' source of values, as a family may practise and follow the values espoused by a particular religion. Once again, the questions of implicit and explicit values may be raised.

The experience of a group of people – a family, community, town, region, or even a country – may give rise to certain values. For example, a country that has a history of civil war, famine or colonisation will certainly value certain things more than others. Peace, a healthy crop and ownership of land may be values that are strongly held in these places. It is difficult to find a source of values in society that is completely untouched by religion, even if it is in active rejection of religious values. Yet we can see that there are secular sources of values in contemporary society. Some of these find resonance and agreement with the major world religions, while others are in conflict with the values of these traditions.

Religion and Secular Culture

Contemporary society is notable for how deeply secular it has become. Never before in human history has there been such a marked decline in religious awareness. However, religion has not disappeared from our world. The great questions of life are still with us. People still respond to these questions with a religious perspective. Alongside this are the secular responses to these questions. The religious and the secular coexist in contemporary society. Sometimes they engage in dialogue; for example, the major religions will comment on upcoming legislation if they judge that it will affect the moral choices of their members. The Irish Catholic Bishops have met with the Government on proposed legislation in Europe regarding stem-cell research; because of the Catholic concern for human life, this was judged to be an issue on which the Church should speak. Through its various organisations, the Catholic Church in Ireland also makes a submission to the Government on the budget. The religious imperative to care for the needy in society, to work for justice in the world and to be mindful of the earth's resources is behind this interaction. Some of the values of modern secular society, such as equality, human rights, education rights and environmental awareness find resonance and agreement in the religious world view. Within Christianity, for example, there is a rich tradition of stewardship and care for the earth. From this tradition comes a deep concern for justice for all humanity. In these areas, secular and religious institutions can work together.

Label Makers

Life is like heady wine. Everyone reads the label on the bottle. Hardly anyone tastes the wine.

Buddha once held up a flower to his disciples and asked each of them to say something about it.
One pronounced a lecture. Another a poem. Yet another a parable. Each trying to outdo the other in depth and erudition. Mahakashyap smiled and said nothing. Only he had seen the flower.

If I could taste a bird, a flower, a tree, a human face! But, alas, I have no time! My energy is spent deciphering the label

Anthony de Mello[50]

Assignments

1. In pairs, research and compare the views held by religious and secular institutions on one of the issues listed below. Some examples of institutions have been provided but these are by no means exhaustive.
- Education – Department of Education and Science, Conference of Religious in Ireland (CORI)
- Housing – Simon, Threshold, Focus Point
- Employment – CORI, Department of Social Welfare, Fás
- Disability – Cope, Centre for Independent Living, L'Arche, Enable Ireland
- Medical research – The Conference of Irish Bishops, Department of Health, Irish Medical Organisation.
- Moral issues – Amnesty International, Crosscare, Trócaire, Concern, Irish Conference of Bishops

2. Write a letter to the president of the European Parliament in which you state your view on the inclusion of a reference to 'God' or 'Christian values' in the European Constitution. State why you take this position and what you think the implications would be if it were otherwise.

There are times when the values of a religious world view come into conflict with the values of society. In these cases religion acts as an alternative view; it becomes '**counter-cultural**'. In a society where image, money and material goods are a measure of success, religion offers an alternative way of measuring human worth. In a society obsessed with dominance and violence, a religion seeks to offer a different vision. The relationship between Church and State is a question that is being worked out across Europe and one that every nation must consider. At the time of writing this text, there is an ongoing debate about the place of God in the European Constitution. Some want a reference to God and Christianity in the Constitution; others do not. It is a debate that could have begun in the Enlightenment, when the religious and secular world views first began their dialogue.

In summary

- The Renaissance, the Enlightenment and the growth of existentialism were key moments in the development of a secular world.

- A secular world view does not look for meaning outside of the person and has created values that may be at odds with religious convictions.

- The feminist movement and the family are examples of sources of secular values.

- Religion and secular culture often clash but they also have common concerns.

Oral/Written Revision of Important Terms

Look up the following terms which you have come across in **bold** type this chapter and briefly explain each one: **secular, secularism, Renaissance, 'liberty, equality and fraternity', feminism, family, counter-cultural.**

Notes

1. David Tuohy and Penny Cairns, *Youth 2K*, Marino Books, 2000, p.2.
2. Niall MacMonagle (ed.), *Real Cool Poems to Grow Up With*, Marino Books, 1994, p.10.
3. Ibid., p.15.
4. Tom Beaudoin, *Virtual Faith, The Irreverent Spiritual Quest of Generation X*, Jossey Bass Wiley, 1998, p.133.
5. Father Brian D'Arcy, *A Little Bit of Hope*, Campus Publishing, 1993, p.36.
6. Joy Carol, *Journeys of Courage*, Veritas, 2003, pp.76-80.
7. Jostein Gaarder, *Sophie's World*, Orion Books, 1997, pp.12-13.
8. Ibid., p.70.
9. Adapted from Frederick Copleston, *History of Philosophy*, Continuum International Publishing Group, 2003, Vol. I, p.287ff.
10. Adapted from Daniel J. Sullivan, *An Introduction to Philosophy*, Macmillan, 1964, p.249ff.
11. Eoin Cassidy, *Into the Classroom: The Search for Meaning and Values*, Veritas, 2004.
12. Jostein Gaarder, *Sophie's World*, Orion Books, 1997, p.220.
13. Quoted and adapted from Robert Graves, *Greek Myths*, Penguin Books, 1993, pp.56-7.
14. Joseph Campbell, *The Hero With A Thousand Faces*, Fontana Press, 1988, pp.185-8.
15. Mircea Eliade, *The Sacred and The Profane*, Columba University Press, 1992, p.37.
16. Terri J. Andrews, *Share in the Light: Native American Stories of Creation*, www.worldandi.com/public/
17. See Paul G. Bahn, *The Story of Archaeology*, Cambridge University Press, 1999, p.11
18. Adapted from Brendan Purcell, MDI, 'Notes for a philosophy of the Human Person'.
19. Riane Eisler, *The Chalice and the Blade*, Harper San Francisco, 1988, p.2.
20. Ibid, p.2.
21. See Michael Drumm, *Passage to Pasch*, Columba Press, 2003, p.20.
22. Eileen Good, *Lough Derg*, Veritas, 2003, pp.1-2.
23. David Tuohy and Penny Cairns, *Youth 2K*, p.35.
24. See Michael Rosen, Karl Marx, in E. Craig (ed.), *Routledge Encyclopaedia of Philosophy*, available on www.rep.routledge.com/article/DCO51
25. See Eoin Cassidy at www.materdei.ie/logos/
26. See Paul Davies, *God and the New Physics*, Penguin Science, 1990.
27. Ibid.
28. Jostein Gaarder, *Sophie's World*, Orion Books, 1997, pp.465-6.
29. Nanci Griffith, 'From a Distance', from the album *Lone Star State of Mind*.
30. Bob Marley, 'Redemption Song' from the album *One Love*, 2001.
31. Adapted from Robert Graves, *Greek Myths*, Penguin Books, 1993, pp.16-20.
32. Jostein Gaarder, *Sophie's World*, Orion Books, 1997, pp.21-2.
33. Ibid, p.23.
34. Quoted in *RE News*, the magazine of the Dublin Post-Primary Diocesan Advisers.
35. Patrick Kavanagh, *The Great Hunger VI*.
36. Documents of Vatican II, *Gaudium et spes*, n.45.
37. Peter McVerry SJ, *The Meaning is in the Shadows*, Veritas, 2003.
38. Anthony De Mello, *Writings Selected by Wm Dych, SJ*, p.45.
39. John Shea, *The Hour of the Unexpected*, Argus Communications, 1997, p.72.
40. John O'Donohue, *Anam Cara*, Bantam Press, 1999, pp.275-6.
41. Bonaventure, *The Journey of the Mind to God*, quoted in Karen Armstrong, *A History God*, Vintage, 1999, p.240.
42. Ibid.
43. Isaac Newton, *Philosophiae Naturalis Principia Mathematica*, quoted in Karen Armstrong, op. cit., p.349.
44. *Gaudium et spes*, n.41; *Ad gentes*, n.9.
45. Gwilym Beckerlegge (ed.), *The World Religions Reader*, Tayler & Francis, 2000, p.1
46. Adapted from Eoin Cassidy, *Challenges to Faith*, www.materdei.ie/logos/Challenges, with the author's permission.
47. Christoph Delius, Matthias Gatzemeier, Deniz Sertcan and Kathleen Wunscher, *The Story of Philosophy from Antiquity to the Present*, p.62.
48. See http://www.yale.edu/lawweb/avalon/rightsof.htm: prepared by Gerald Mur (The Cleveland Free-Net).
49. Ibid.
50. Anthony De Mello, *Writings Selected by Wm Dych SJ*, Mary Knoll, New York, p.50.